LOVE YOUR *UNBORN* NEIGHBOUR

LOVE YOUR *UNBORN* NEIGHBOUR

SPUC
London
1994

First published in Great Britain in 1994 by
The Society for the Protection of Unborn Children

ISBN 1 898864 00 4

British Library Cataloguing in Publication Data.
A catalogue record for this book is available from the British Library.

Picture credits:

Cover photograph and p. 19: Science Photo Library

Frontispiece and photographs on pages 8, 71, 75, 93, 111, 113, 115, 131, 139, 141, 144, 147, 149 by Carlos Reyes-Manzo of the Andes Press Agency.

Other photographs as follows: page 13 by Mick Rock, reproduced by courtesy of CARE; page 22 by *The Independent*; page 54 by *The Irish Times*; page 69 by Guzelian; page 95 by The Press Association; page 123 by Robert Whelan.

Portrait of William Wilberforce by Sir Thomas Lawrence on page 33 reproduced by courtesy of The National Portrait Gallery, London.

Engravings on pages viii, xi, 1 (facing), 6, 9, 137 and 153 by Gustave Doré for *La Sainte Bible*, published Alfred Mame et fils, Tours, France (1865).

Unless otherwise stated, scriptural quotations are taken from the HOLY BIBLE, NEW INTERNATIONAL VERSION © 1973, 1978, 1984 by International Bible Society. Used by permission.

Book Production by Crowley Esmonde Ltd
Typeset by Goodfellow & Egan, Cambridge
Printed by Hillman Printers (Frome) Ltd
Bound by Woolnough Bookbinding Ltd

Contents

Rescue those being led away to death;
hold back those staggering towards slaughter.
If you say, 'But we knew nothing about this,'
does not he who weighs the heart perceive it?
Does not he who guards your life know it?
Will he not repay each person according to what he has done?

Proverbs 24:11–12

The unborn child and obedience to God

This book is primarily a plea from evangelicals to evangelicals, although it will be of interest to many others. We would ask those who accept the authority of the Bible, who love God and long to obey God, to look at what is happening to unborn children in our country (and indeed around the world) in the light of Scripture. What should the response of the Lord's own people be?

Faith

Justification by faith alone stands at the heart of evangelical doctrine. Yet from end to end the Scripture assures us that faith is far more than mere mental assent or an orthodox creed: true and saving faith results in changed lives and obedience to God.

Right faith must issue in right conduct.

James, in his letter, calls the sort of faith that falls short of this 'dead' and reminds us that even the demons have that sort. He points out that Abraham's faith held nothing back in obedience to God; Rahab's meant coming to the aid of those in great danger. This is the faith that counts for righteousness.

The righteous will indeed live by faith, but John points out in his first letter that 'Whoever claims to live in him must walk as Jesus did' (1 John 2:6).

Paul, the great expositor of justification by faith, repeatedly concludes his teaching of doctrine with an ethical exhortation – for right faith must issue in right conduct.

Jesus himself said, 'Now that you know these things, you will be blessed if you do them' (John 13:17). In his striking description of the final judgement in the simile of the sheep and the goats he confirms that the righteous will certainly have given help to those in great need; the rest will have failed in this duty.

If we believe that we are justified by faith, it should cause us concern when an outward profession of faith is not accompanied by a life conformed to God's will. Not that we look for perfection, but for evidence that what is professed is genuine, saving faith. Failure in such basic things as respect for human life or protection of the innocent from violence is clear evidence to the contrary.

Facing page: The trial of Abraham's faith.

Hope

In the last quarter of a century the pro-life movement has made great advances, both in this country and in other parts of the world.

The educational work of the The Society for the Protection of Unborn Children (SPUC) and other organisations means that many more people now recognise and understand the humanity of the unborn child and have grasped the horror of what happens to unborn children through abortion and experimentation. The lives of many children have been saved by this educational work.

Of course there are reverses as well as successes. In Britain, in spite of strong support from many MPs, front-bench hostility has thwarted attempts to improve the legal position. The British abortion legislation has also been used as a model in many other countries.

The struggle to gain protection for unborn children may sometimes appear to be a lost cause and this impression is certainly encouraged by the distorted and tendentious presentation of the subject in our mass media – the only source of information for many people.

Our struggle is not against flesh and blood.

Christians should not be perplexed by the apparent triumph of evil over good. Scripture makes clear that the forces of evil in this world are powerful and destructive. Our duty as servants of Christ is to stand boldly in the spiritual battle, equipped and protected by the full armour of God; for our struggle is not against flesh and blood (Eph. 6:12–18).

We make this stand with confidence. Our hope is fixed not on the successes of the pro-life movement to date, nor on its gathering momentum among Christians; we put our hope in the living God. For God's word not only proclaims the sanctity of every human life as the bedrock of society, it also assures us that the Saviour whom we serve has triumphed over the forces of evil and that the final victory is already his.

Scripture tells of numerous people who, in this hope, opposed obediently and with vigour the evils of their own day. They did so even though their vision of final vindication was seen only dimly, 'as through a dark glass'. The same is true of many more recent figures in the evangelical heritage. William Wilberforce, for example, devoted his life to the suppression of slavery, one of 'two great objects' which, he said, 'God has set before me'. In this costly battle, against entrenched opposition, Wilberforce was sustained by his daily communing with God, in whose will he sought to live. This work of half a century ended with the emancipation of slaves throughout the British Empire: Wilber-

THE UNBORN CHILD AND OBEDIENCE TO GOD xi

force heard the news of Parliament's decision on his deathbed.

We have our cloud of witnesses.

Love

Our whole duty towards others is summed up in the second great commandment: 'Love your neighbour as yourself'. We cannot evade the fact that this is what we are commanded to do – it is not optional.

Commitment to the pro-life cause is sometimes seen as a valid and laudable option for those with a particular concern for personal morality or an interest in ethical questions concerning human reproduction. This is an inadequate view. Defence of the unborn, victims of the greatest outrage in our society, is a requirement not an option.

It is a requirement implicit in the commandment to love our neighbour. When Jesus was asked 'And who is my neighbour?' he replied with a famous parable (Luke 10: 30–37). The example of the good Samaritan in obeying this commandment shows us two things in particular about the meaning of love.

Defence of the unborn is a requirement not an option.

First, love is not bound by contemporary ideas of who is (or is not) a neighbour. The Jews of Jesus' day despised Samaritans and would certainly not think of them as 'neighbours'. They treated Samaritans atrociously (similar treatment was returned), but would not have thought of this as failing to love their neighbour. The parable shows that they were wrong. Our own society has taken a very similar attitude to unborn children, denying their dignity by the regular use of impersonal terms such as 'fetus' and 'products of conception', and excluding them from the protection that the law gives to everyone else. Our obedience to God cannot be bound by this prejudicial attitude. We must love the neighbour whom society spurns.

Second, love meets the needs our neighbour presents to us. The shocking thing about the priest and the Levite in the parable was their total disregard for the man whose plight was clear to them. They were in a position to help, but did not. In our society no group suffers a more terrible plight than unborn children. Their sufferings compare with the worst to be found around the world, both in degree (deliberate and brutal killing) and scale (at least one in five of all children conceived in the UK are aborted) and yet our society ignores them, passing by on the other side. If we are to obey the commandment, we must come to the aid of those in our midst whose need is so great and whom we have the power to help. Love is not a matter of mere words, it requires action (1 John 3:18). Jesus said 'Go and do likewise'.

*   *   *

The shame and tragedy of our recent history have been the failure of the Church, by and large, to help the unborn. With uneasy conscience we have watched as the unthinkable and the unspeakable have unfolded before our eyes.

The injustices of British law were not challenged. Government was not reminded of its indispensable duty, ordained by God, to preserve justice in a fallen society. The medical community was not warned of its guilt in harbouring the takers of life. Church leaders who condoned and advocated the killing were not exposed. Mothers and their families were not cared for with compassion and truth.

Christians in this country are deeply implicated in the guilt of our society. Called by Christ to be his witnesses, we have been compromised in our preaching of the Gospel by our disobedience. Our message of reconciliation has been discredited because we have forgotten one of its basic premises: the value of human life in God's eyes.

This book has been produced in the hope that the eyes of Christians will be opened to the truth, appalling as it is, and that the Church will repent of its disobedience. God's word lies open to us:

Christians in this country are deeply implicated in the guilt of our society.

> . . . if my people, who are called by my name, will humble themselves and pray and seek my face and turn from their wicked ways, then will I hear from heaven and will forgive their sin and will heal their land.
>
> *2 Chronicles 7:14*

May God have mercy on us yet.

Steven Foster
Chairman, SPUC Evangelicals

CHAPTER ONE

The Church and the unborn child

He who has an ear, let him hear what the Spirit says to the churches.
Revelation 3:6

Setting the Scene

> The whole counsel of God concerning all things necessary for His glory, man's salvation, faith and life, is either expressly set down in Scripture, or by good and necessary consequence may be deduced from Scripture.
>
> *Westminster Confession* (1648)[1]

In the Bible we see a continuous witness to the sanctity of human life.

The Scriptures, to which the Westminster Confession directs the attention of the believing Christian, are the foundation of all that we will want to say about the unborn child and the stand which the believer must take on such issues as abortion and embryo research. In the Bible and in the witness of the Christian community from its earliest days down to this present century we see a continuous and united witness to the sanctity of human life in God's eyes and the responsibility and duty laid on God's faithful people to respect and defend that life.

However, we may not look to the Bible for slick solutions to current controversial problems. What we can find are God-given principles of thought and action. These we must absorb to inform our conscience and develop a Christian mind. In this way we can make judgements on the topics of the day.

What does the Bible say?

It is at first sight surprising that in the whole of the Bible there is no really clear text that condemns abortion. It is more surprising when one realises that ancient laws of the surrounding nations could be very harsh on those causing the loss of an unborn child, for example the Middle Assyrian law:

Facing page:
The Annunciation.

If a woman by her own deed cast out that which is in her, and a charge has been brought and proved against her, they shall impale her and not bury her.[2]

It has been suggested that the reason for this is that abortion was not an issue with the Jewish nation in Old Testament times; the real issue affecting the very young was the human sacrifices to pagan deities.

The fact that Assyrian law has no parallel in the Pentateuch is not evidence that abortion was considered acceptable. M. J. Gorman concludes from his study of the writings of the Jews that in all the known Jewish literature up to AD 500 we have no record of an abortion which was not carried out to preserve the mother's life. The Talmud, that vast collection of rabbinic teaching over hundreds of years, only refers to to one abortion for any other reason, and this is 'almost certainly' the doing of a non-Jew (it is, of course, condemned). Gorman continues:

'Jews, unlike pagans, did not practice deliberate abortion.'

It was a given of Jewish thought and life that abortion, like exposure, was unacceptable, and this was well known in the ancient world . . . Jews, unlike pagans, did not practice deliberate abortion.[3]

This is confirmed in the writings of the Jewish historian, Josephus:

The law forbids women either to cause abortion or to make away with the foetus; a woman convicted of this is regarded as an infanticide.[4]

The Exodus text
There is one specific text to which we must give some attention. Rex Gardner in *Abortion: The Personal Dilemma* says of Exodus 21:22–25 that 'there is only one clear reference to abortion in the Old Testament, and this refers to accidental miscarriage'.[5]

If men who are fighting hit a pregnant woman and she gives birth prematurely but there is no serious injury, the offender must be fined whatever the woman's husband demands and the court allows. But if there is serious injury, you are to take life for life, eye for eye, tooth for tooth, hand for hand, foot for foot, burn for burn, wound for wound, bruise for bruise.

Exodus 21:22–25

Neither the actual text nor its interpretation are very clear. It deals with the legal penalty in the case of a fight between men which results in injury to a woman bystander who is pregnant. Interpretation depends on the phrase 'if there is serious injury' in verse 23. Injury to whom? One interpretation is to take both mother and child as possible victims of harm; the other leaves the child out of the account.

But even if we assume the second interpretation to be the true one (and what we read elsewhere in the Bible suggests we accept the first) we are not reading about the punishment for deliberately induced abortion. We are considering the punishment for an accidental injury as a by-product of a quarrel between two men, neither of whom even knew that the woman would be hurt, never mind that she was with child.

A deliberate attack on a pregnant woman is a particularly heinous crime, being the sin for which Ammon is condemned in the time of Amos:

> For three sins of Ammon,
> even for four, I will not turn back my wrath.
> Because he ripped open the pregnant woman of Gilead
> in order to extend his borders.
>
> *Amos 1:13*

The evil king Menahem was also guilty of this offence (2 Kings 15:16) as was Hazael (2 Kings 8:12).

The sanctity of human life

Let us now return to the quotation from Josephus. He says that abortion is the same as infanticide, equal to the killing of a child after it has been born. The Didache is even clearer saying 'You shall not slay the child by abortion'.[6] What both writers are in effect saying is that abortion is not some new crime which requires legislation nor some new sin to add to those already proscribed in the Commandments. They are saying that the Bible already condemns abortion because it condemns murder. Abortion is a sort of special case to which the sixth commandment applies.

Children are clearly covered by the prohibition of killing in the sixth commandment.

Time and time again the Bible speaks of children before birth in terms that imply that it treats them simply as very young children. If this is the case then such children are clearly covered by the prohibition of killing in the sixth commandment. Therefore we must look at some of these sections of the Bible in detail.

First, though, we need to set it all out in the context of the doctrine of creation. Man, Scripture attests and Christian creeds affirm, is made in the image and likeness of God. It is this which sets men, women and children apart from the rest of creation and gives human life a unique value and sanctity. The creation narratives in Genesis make this clear (see Genesis 1:26–27; 5:1–2) and in Genesis 9:6, where murder is forbidden, we read that it is because of this image:

'In the image of God has God made man.'

> Whoever sheds the blood of man,
> by man shall his blood be shed;
> for in the image of God
> has God made man.

Unborn children in the Bible

The clearest and most important references to unborn children are to be found in the early chapters of St Luke's Gospel, perhaps doubly significant since Luke was a doctor. So we may have not only theological but medical and scientific statements combined. This is not to suggest that Luke had advance knowledge of the modern understanding of fetology but it is not beyond the bounds of belief that this Spirit-filled writer was by divine guidance allowed to see in some way what we can now confirm (see Chapter 2).

Before the birth of John the Baptist the angel promises that he will be filled with the Holy Spirit from his mother's womb (Luke 1:15). When Elizabeth is six months pregnant she is visited by Mary who has just conceived. The tiny Jesus in his mother's womb causes the Spirit-filled John to leap with joy (Luke 1:41–44). While we cannot begin to understand these mysteries fully it is clear that the Bible is saying that this unborn child, John, is in the full sense a human person, made in the divine image, and capable of being pressed into the divine service for a distinct purpose, to witness to the Son of God.

While the unborn John recognised Jesus in his actions his mother Elizabeth spoke to Mary: 'Why am I so favoured, that the mother of my Lord should come to me?' (Luke 1:43). By calling Mary the mother of her Lord Elizabeth acknowledges the unborn Jesus as her Lord already. It is also worth noting that throughout this narrative Luke uses the Greek word *brephos* for the unborn John, the same word as used by Luke later for the newborn baby Jesus (Luke 2:12,16) and of the little ones people brought for Jesus to bless (Luke 18:15).

We need to go back a little further to get to the heart of this narrative, to Mary's encounter with Gabriel. In dramatic terms we are told of the coming of God in the flesh:

> The Holy Spirit will come upon you, and the power of the Most High will overshadow you.
>
> *Luke 1:35*

This is the moment of the Incarnation (see also Matthew 1:20), as Christians have confessed in the Apostles' Creed for centuries:

> . . . Jesus Christ, his only Son our Lord, who was conceived by the Holy Ghost, born of the Virgin Mary.

The fruit of Mary's conception, when the Spirit 'came upon her' and the 'power of the Most High' overshadowed her, was 'Jesus Christ his only Son, our Lord' so when Elizabeth called Mary 'the mother of my Lord' she was right. Already, in the womb of Mary, the Son of God had taken flesh.

We have then plain evidence for the full continuity of life unborn and born in the case of John and in the supreme case of Jesus Christ. So we can go on to examine other references to unborn children in Scripture to see if there is the same possibility of the activity of God in their lives at this stage. We shall not be disappointed.

The prophet Jeremiah gives vent to his sense of dejection by wishing that he had never been born.

> May he hear wailing in the morning,
>   a battle cry at noon.
> For he did not kill me in the womb,
>   with my mother as my grave,
>   her womb enlarged for ever.
> Why did I ever come out of the womb
>   to see trouble and sorrow
>   and to end my days in shame?
>
> *Jeremiah 20:16–18*

Jeremiah understands his personal existence as going back to the womb.

Clearly the prophet understands his personal existence as going back to the womb. Jeremiah says 'he did not kill me in the womb', and, since he was not killed there, he can talk of coming out of the womb to see the unhappy life which has been his. The personal existence of Jeremiah is therefore clearly established before birth. With birth it continued.

Similar sentiments come from Job:

6 LOVE YOUR UNBORN NEIGHBOUR

> Why then did you bring me out of the womb?
> I wish I had died before any eye saw me.
> If only I had never come into being,
> or had been carried straight from the womb to the grave!
>
> *Job 10:18–19*

The idea in the second sentence is especially interesting. Job (who acknowledges that it was God who fashioned him in the womb – see verses 8–11) seems to envisage two possibilities: that he had never come into being on the one hand, and on the other that he had been stillborn. Thus he implies that the stillborn child has already come into being before it dies.

In the case of Jacob, we find that the struggles with his twin brother Esau, which were a feature of their later life, began in the womb. Jacob was already marked out by God to enjoy his special favour. After their mother, Rebekah, became pregnant, we read that:

> The babies jostled each other within her, and she said, 'Why is this happening to me?' So she went to enquire of the Lord.
> The Lord said to her,
> 'Two nations are in your womb,
> and two peoples from within you will be separated;
> one people will be stronger than the other,
> and the older will serve the younger.'
>
> *Genesis 25:22–23*

In the psalms of David there are several references to life before birth which seem to come to a climax in Psalm 139:

> For you created my inmost being;
> you knit me together in my mother's womb.
> I praise you because I am fearfully and wonderfully made;
> your works are wonderful,
> I know that full well.
> My frame was not hidden from you
> when I was made in the secret place.
> When I was woven together in the depths of the earth,
> your eyes saw my unformed body.
> All the days ordained for me
> were written in your book
> before one of them came to be.
>
> *Psalm 139:13–16*

'You knit me together in my mother's womb.'

In his booklet *Abortion* John Stott talks of three stages in the

development of the themes of this great psalm. First there is the theme of **Creation**:

> . . . you created my inmost being;
> you knit me together in my mother's womb.

While this is not a scientific account of the growth of the embryo the psalmist makes it clear:

> . . . that the process of embryonic growth is neither haphazard nor even automatic, but a divine work of creative skill.[7]

The second theme is **Continuity**. The psalmist is now an adult, but he looks back over his life to the time before he was born. He refers to himself both before and after birth by the same personal pronouns 'I' and 'me'; antenatal and postnatal, he was and is the same person:

> He who is thinking and writing as a grown man has the same personal identity as the foetus in the womb . . . before and after his birth, as embryo, baby, youth and adult, he is conscious of being the same person.[8]

The third and final theme is **Communion** or **Covenant**. The author is aware of a very personal communion between God and himself and, perhaps more accurately, a covenant, since the relationship is something which God has established and God sustains. Stott points out that the 'I–You' relationship is expressed in almost every line.

'There is a complete continuity between life inside and life outside the womb.'

It is these three words (Creation, Continuity and Communion or Covenant) which give us the essential biblical perspective from which to think. The foetus is neither a growth in the mother's body, nor even a potential human being, but already a human being who, though not yet mature, has the potentiality of growing into the fullness of the individual humanity he *already* possesses.[9]

The examples of Jeremiah, Job and the Psalmist confirm the lessons we have already learned from the infancy narratives of Doctor Luke that, as Nigel Cameron and Pamela Simms put it:

Facing page: Job hearing of his ruin.

> . . . there is a complete continuity between life inside and life outside the womb, that the unborn child is regarded as a person, and that the moment of conception is the point at which the

beginning of human life is to be found. In other words, that which constitutes a human person finds its beginning not at birth, nor at some intermediate point during pregnancy and the developing physical form of the fetus, but at the very beginning of the process. The point of conception is the moment at which there comes into existence a person who bears the image of God, who joins in the guilt of his race and who is capable of being filled with the Holy Spirit.[10]

The witness of the Church

In his book *Medical Ethics and Human Life* David Braine shows that:

> For the whole of Christian history until appreciably after 1900, so far as we can trace it, there was virtually complete unanimity amongst Christians . . . that, unless at the direct command of God, it was in all cases wrong directly to take innocent human life.[11]

Acceptance of abortion constitutes failure to maintain the Church's work of proclaiming God's righteous character and will.

Today we are often told that this is a particular issue for one group of Christians, and that it is not all that clear as an issue. But if we really look at the evidence we see that David Braine is right; that certainly until the beginning of this century and even well into it, the idea of abortion's being compatible with Christian belief is non-existent.

This consistent upholding of the sanctity of human life throughout Christian history has, we have seen, been in accordance with the witness of Scripture. Twentieth-century acceptance of abortion therefore constitutes not only departure from a tradition but also failure to maintain the Church's work of proclaiming God's righteous character and will.

The early centuries

Probably the earliest source is The Didache or the Teaching of the Twelve Apostles. At one time this was thought to date from around AD 150 but some now think it could be contemporaneous with St Matthew's Gospel. It stated:

> You shall not kill the child in the womb or murder a new-born infant.[12]

Around AD 177 Athenagoras of Athens wrote:

> We say that those women who use drugs to bring on abortion commit murder and will have to give an account to God for the

abortion . . . For it does not belong to the same person to regard the very fetus in the womb as a created being and therefore an object of God's care, and when it has passed into life, to kill it.[13]

Clement of Alexandria said in AD 195:

But women who resort to some sort of deadly abortion drug kill not only the embryo but, along with it, all human kindness.[14]

John Chrysostom, in Homily XXIV on the Epistle of Paul to the Romans, asked:

Why then dost thou abuse the gift of God, and fight with His laws, and pursue what is a curse as if a blessing, and make the chamber of procreation a chamber of murder, and arm the woman that was given for child-bearing unto slaughter?[15]

Turning to the Fathers of the West, Tertullian in his Apologeticum of AD 197 wrote:

But with us murder is forbidden once and for all. We are not permitted to destroy even the fetus in the womb, as long as blood is still being drawn to form a human being. To prevent the birth of a child is anticipated murder.[16]

The Middle Ages
This attitude displayed by writers from the earliest centuries is continued throughout the Middle Ages. Thomist philosophers often made appeal to Augustine who wrote as follows in respect of abortion:

Sometimes this sexually indulgent cruelty or this cruel sexual indulgence goes so far as to procure potions which produce sterility. If the desired result is not achieved, the mother terminates the life and expels the fetus which was in her womb in such a way that the child dies.[17]

'To prevent the birth of a child is anticipated murder.'

Many of the debates of the Middle Ages were about 'animation' and the status of the unborn. Again Augustine is often quoted:

I fail to see why, if they are not excluded from the number of the dead, they shall not attain to the resurrection of the dead . . . we must at least apply to them, if they rise again, all that we have to say of infants who have been born.[18]

The Reformation

The turmoil of the sixteenth century led to many breaks with the thinking of the past. Much that was considered corrupt and especially at variance with the witness of the Bible was rejected and overturned. However, on the issue of the unborn and abortion there is remarkable continuity.

> Early Protestant attitudes to abortion show considerable continuity with those of the pre-sixteenth century Church ... The reformers insisted upon the full humanity of the foetus from the time of conception.[19]

A quotation from the writings of John Calvin amply illustrates the validity of this general point:

> The fetus, though enclosed in the womb of its mother, is already a human being ... If it seems more horrible to kill a man in his own house than in a field, because a man's house is his place of most secure refuge, it ought surely to be deemed more atrocious to destroy a fetus in the womb before it has come to light.[20]

Modern times

In modern times the public perception is that opposition to abortion on Christian grounds comes from the Roman Catholic community. While we must thank that church for its firmness on this issue of life and death we must not ignore the fact that others have also stood firm in the biblical and traditional belief. Nor should we be unaware of the fact that, as Bernard Nathanson explained in *Aborting America*, it is a tactic of the pro-abortion lobby to identify this as a Roman Catholic issue and thus isolate those who defend life.

'The fetus is already a human being.'

> Our movement persistently tarred all opposition with the brush of the Roman Catholic Church or its hierarchy, stirring up anti-Catholic prejudices, and pontificated about the necessity for 'separation of church and state' ... All of this religious line was, of course, necessary political strategy.[21]

Two protestant theologians of the twentieth century, Dietrich Bonhoeffer and Karl Barth, may therefore end our kaleidoscope of quotations:

> Destruction of the embryo in the mother's womb is a violation of the right to live which God has bestowed ... The simple fact is that God certainly intended to create a human being and that

this nascent human being has been deliberately deprived of his life. And that is nothing but murder.[22]

This child is a man for whose life the Son of God died . . . The true light of the world shines already in the darkness of the mother's womb. And yet they want to kill him deliberately because certain reasons which have nothing to do with the child himself favour the view that he had better not be born![23]

Nigel Cameron noted the witness given in recent years by evangelical Christians when he wrote:

Perhaps the most striking feature of the campaign for David Alton's Bill was the fact that much of the public support for this brave young Roman Catholic M.P. came from Evangelicals. CARE sponsored a series of meetings and the largest of these filled the Royal Albert Hall . . . Most of the 5,000 people present were Evangelicals; Clive Calver of the Evangelical Alliance was one of a series of speakers and I was another.[24]

Conclusion

The clear evidence of the Bible and the united witness of the Christian Church through the centuries point us to the fact that God made all human beings in his image and likeness and lead us to the conclusion that direct abortion is contrary to his revealed will.

The silence of the churches in the debates of the 1960s which led to our present law must be replaced with their outspoken witness. As the tide of faith has ebbed, values have been discarded. Abortion is a sign of the times and the prophetic voice of the people of God must see this sign and speak in God's name to this generation.

The prophetic voice of the people of God must speak in God's name to this generation.

CHAPTER TWO

You knit me together

For you created my inmost being;
you knit me together in my mother's womb.
Psalm 139:13

Life is a miracle! It is easy to take human life for granted and to forget the miraculous sequence of events that goes to make each person what he is. Each person is unique, loved and absolutely priceless in the eyes of our Maker – Almighty God.

It is important to see the stages that each human being passes through in the first nine months of existence and to realise the wonder of our creation. However, it is sobering to reflect that in many countries of the world, and certainly in Britain today, the womb is the most dangerous place for a child to be. Because of abortion, human beings are at greater risk of violent death during the first nine months of their lives than at any subsequent stage.

Human beings are at greater risk of violent death during the first nine months of their lives than at any subsequent stage.

Let us discover human life in its earliest stages by following the development of a baby girl in the first nine months of her life.

The first month

The beginning of life for each human being is **fertilisation**, when the father's sperm fertilises the mother's egg. This momentous event is the beginning of a completely new human being – similar to and yet different from both the mother and the father. Unique in her own right from fertilisation, the new human is different in kind and nature from the sperm and egg that have combined to create her. Many of the characteristics of the new individual are determined at conception or fertilisation – the colour of hair, eyes and skin, the sex and factors which influence height and build.

The new human is in control of the pregnancy, not the mother. Her growth is controlled by her own genetic code or DNA. The cells of living beings contain DNA (deoxyribonucleic acid). This is the complex substance that enables cells to reproduce and transmit characteristics from one generation to another. Dr Margaret White in her book *Two Million Silent Killings* describes DNA like this:

> A single thread of DNA from a human cell contains information equivalent to over half a million pages with five hundred words to a page, or a library containing a thousand volumes!

Dr White then quotes Dr Hymie Gordon, Chief Geneticist at the Mayo Clinic, USA, who says:

> From the moment of fertilisation when the deoxyribonucleic acids from the spermatozoon [sperm] and the ovum [egg] come together to form the zygote [the new one-celled being after fertilisation], the pattern of the individual's constitutional development is irrevocably determined . . . True, environmental influences, both during the intra-uterine period and after birth, modify the individual's constitution and continue to do so right until his death, but it is at conception that the individual's capacity to respond to these . . . influences is established.[1] [Words in brackets added.]

Fertilisation normally takes place in the fallopian tube which connects the womb (where the baby will have her home for nine months) to the ovary (where the mother's egg has come from). The womb is a large flexible muscle which stretches to allow for the baby's growth throughout pregnancy.

The next stage of development is **implantation**. Following fertilisation the single cell splits into two, four and so on. This process is called **differentiation** – when the cells organise themselves into different parts and functions. The number of cells is growing constantly. The journey along the fallopian tube continues for about four days until the tiny human being reaches the womb.

'A single thread of DNA contains information equivalent to a library containing a thousand volumes.'

Since fertilisation has taken place, the lining of the womb has been preparing itself for its new inhabitant. It has formed a soft, spongy lining into which the embryo (as she is now called) burrows and makes her home. This process of implantation begins six days after fertilisation and is complete within the next week.

If implantation does not take place then the lining of the womb comes away at the end of the woman's monthly cycle. However, if implantation occurs the embryo sends out a hormonal signal which stops the mother's next period. This is

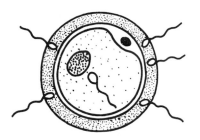

Day 1: Fertilisation. 0.14mm

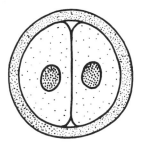

Day 2: Zygote divides. 0.14mm

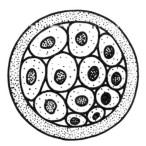

Day 3: Morula. 0.14mm

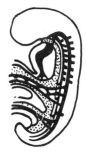

Day 22: Heart starts to beat. 2.0mm

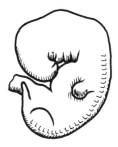

Day 29: Crown to rump. 5.0mm

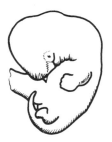

Day 35: Crown to rump. 12.0–14.0mm

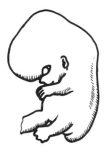

Day 42: Crown to rump. 23.0–23.5mm

when she has the first idea that she is pregnant and that a new life has well and truly begun!

While implantation is happening the embryo develops a covering or capsule (the amnion) around herself that is filled with fluid. This acts as a protective covering which prevents injury. The outer membrane is called the chorion, part of which forms the placenta. The placenta is a vital organ for the growing baby. It transfers nutrients from the mother's bloodstream and removes waste from the child. The bloodstream of mother and baby remain completely separate. The placenta also produces hormones to maintain the pregnancy. It plays a crucial role in the process of labour, although how labour begins is still poorly understood.

The baby is attached to the placenta by the umbilical cord. This is the lifeline that channels nutrients and waste between the mother and the child. The child obtains oxygen from the mother's blood via the umbilical cord and the placenta during the pregnancy.

Twenty-five days after fertilisation the child's body is beginning to develop. The head and trunk appear and the arm buds. Between 21 and 25 days the baby's heart begins to beat and other internal organs are beginning to form. The late Sir William Liley, known as the Father of Fetology, described this early stage of the child's development like this:

Between 21 and 25 days the baby's heart begins to beat.

> By 30 days, just two weeks past mother's first missed period, the baby – one quarter of an inch long – has a brain of unmistakable human proportions . . . mouth, kidneys, liver, an umbilical cord and a heart pumping blood he has made himself.[2]

The second month

The embryo grows from 5 millimetres at four weeks to 40 millimetres at the end of the eighth week. By the sixth week from fertilisation tiny fingers appear, followed within days by toes. At the same time the eyes develop the lens and retina and the eyelids begin to appear. Brain waves can also be detected.

At seven weeks the child has her own fingerprints, the outer ear is present, and the inner ear, with its hearing and balancing mechanisms, is well established. A British study has shown that the child's movements begin at the same time as sensory nerves begin to grow into the spinal cord during the second month of pregnancy. The study concluded that the baby's sensory nerves 'appear to be more sensitive than those of the adult or newborn baby'.[3]

At about eight weeks the baby's skeleton begins to turn from cartilage to bone.

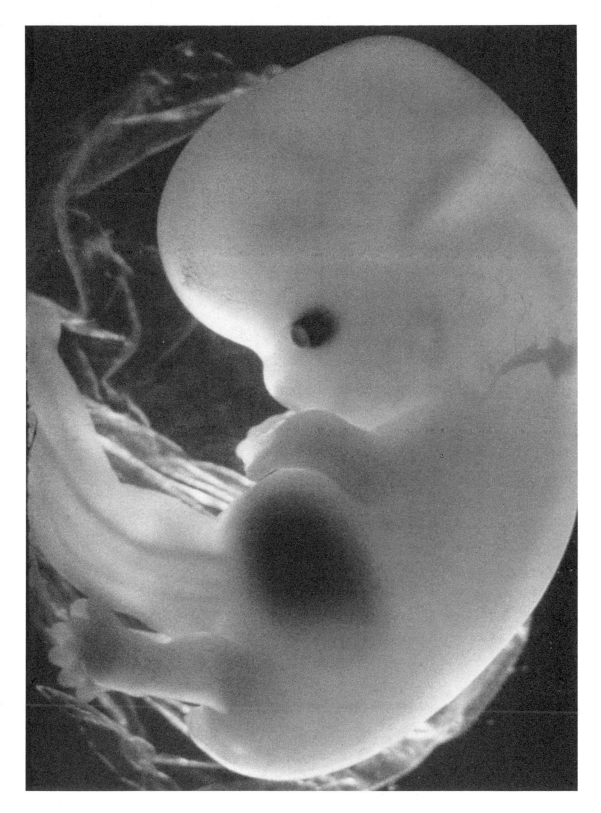

The third month

At 12 weeks the child's features are becoming more defined. The unborn baby can open or close the lips, wrinkle the forehead, raise the eyebrows and turn the head. The baby's sex is easy to determine by now. The baby measures about 90 millimetres and weighs 45 grams. She is also sensitive to touch. A report in the *British Medical Journal* states that:

> Nine weeks after conception the baby is well enough formed to bend his fingers round an object in the palm of his hand. In response to a touch on the sole of his foot he will curl his toes or bend his hips and knees to move away from the touching object. At 12 weeks he can close his fingers and thumb and will open his mouth in response to pressure applied at the base of the thumb ... At 11 weeks after conception the fetus starts to swallow the surrounding amniotic fluid and to pass it back in his urine. He can also produce complex facial expressions and even smile.[4]

'The first trimester fetus may be more susceptible to pain than slightly older subjects.'

The child can also feel pain. Brain cells essential for consciousness in the adult are present in the 10-week-old fetus. The nerve fibres which transmit pain are present before the nerve fibres inhibiting pain are developed. In his book *The Fetus as Transplant Donor* Peter McCullach has commented that:

> this implies that the first trimester fetus may be more susceptible to pain than slightly older subjects.[5]

This is the stage of development at which abortions are most frequently performed.

The fourth and fifth months

At 16 weeks the baby is a little over one third of the size she will be at birth, weighing approximately 200 grams. The heart pumps 30 litres of blood every day. There is also evidence to suggest that from four months onwards the child can hear and is sensitive to light. The report quoted earlier from the *British Medical Journal* records that:

> In fact, the inner ear of the fetus is completely developed by mid-pregnancy, and the fetus responds to a wide variety of sounds. He is surrounded by a constant very loud noise in the uterus – the rhythmical sound of the uterine blood supply punctuated by the noises of air passing through the mother's intestine. Loud noises from outside the uterus such as the

slamming of a door or loud music reach the fetus and he reacts to them.[6]

Unborn children are also sensitive to music and display certain distinct tastes. It has been noted that different types of music produce different responses. For example:

> A four- or five-month-old foetus definitely responds to sound and melody – and responds in very discriminating ways. Put Vivaldi on the record player and even the most agitated baby relaxes.[7]

Babies also learn to recognise their mother's voice in the womb.

New-born babies whose mothers watched 'Neighbours' during pregnancy have been seen to stop crying and become alert when they hear the theme tune after birth.[8]

From the sixteenth week babies are also sensitive to light. When a light is shone on to the mother's womb, the child's heartbeat changes.[9]

The fifth month to birth

During the last months of pregnancy up to birth the baby continues to grow and gain weight. At 20 weeks she will weigh about 460 grams. Hair, eyebrows, eyelashes and nails are growing. The baby will also receive the mother's antibodies against infection until her own immune system is developed, and will wake and sleep and be sensitive to the mother's moods and emotions.

When the baby is born she has already been alive for nine months. What changes at birth is the baby's environment, not her status as a human being.

Created by God

Remarkable as the process of human development in the womb is, as Christians we cannot suppose that a purely physical account of our early life is the whole story. As the apostle Paul puts it, 'From now on we regard no one from a worldly point of view' (2 Cor. 5:16). So what can we say about the spiritual significance of the baby whose awesome physical development we have just described?

The care of God

The entire process is, of course, overseen and directed by a loving God. Whether or not we are aware of the new baby growing and maturing, whether or not we care, God is

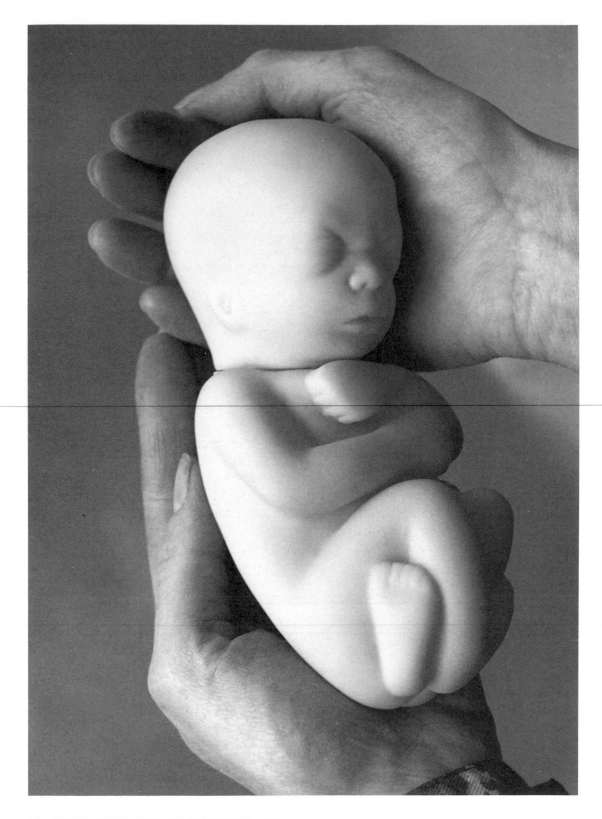

22   LOVE YOUR UNBORN NEIGHBOUR

fashioning every new part and directing every development with infinite care. This intimate involvement of the Creator in the process of human growth in the womb is beautifully described in Psalm 139, as we saw on pp.7–8.

Facing page: A life-sized model of the unborn child at 18 weeks after conception.

The image of God

The growing child is distinctively human from the beginning of her life at conception. As a human being she shares with the rest of us in the human race a special status and value which sets us apart from the rest of creation.

The first thing that is said about human beings in the Bible is that they are made in the image of God. Male and female are each bearers of the divine image:

> So God created man in his own image,
> in the image of God he created him;
> male and female he created them.
>
> *Genesis 1:27*

What does this say about the species *homo sapiens*? First, it can be said that to bear the image of the Creator is to have a high value conferred upon the species. Indeed, God has placed privileges and responsibilities upon the people who bear his image. Their responsibility is to rule the earth within the bounds the Creator has set. The great privilege is to have a special relationship with the Creator himself that is accorded to no other species. This image-bearing is different from the image that is borne in a portrait. That is static; it displays no growth or movement. The image of God in a human person is moving, growing, creative – indeed like the Creator himself.

The Bible nowhere defines what it means to be made 'in the image of God'. However, certain human characteristics can be seen to mirror our Creator, though by reason of our frailty and sin only in part and imperfectly. For example, the human faculties of reason, conscience and freewill all reflect godly characteristics: the ability to think beyond the purely instinctive, the knowledge of right and wrong and the ability to choose independently. The image of God may also be seen in the capacity for relationships with other human beings and, supremely, with God himself through Christ, and in the ability to love other human beings and God, which is a reflection of God's love for his creatures.

It is human beings who have shaped our world. Why is this? It is certainly not because of their physical prowess – for many animal species are much stronger than we are. It is not because,

The image of God in a human person is moving, growing, creative.

numerically, humans are so great and populate vast tracts of the planet. Essentially men and women have ordered the world to meet their needs because they are made *in the image of God*. That is to say, God has endowed them with the heavenly gifts of reason, self-awareness and foresight. They can choose between different courses of action, just as they can choose between right and wrong. They are the creators of their own environment, not the victims of it, like the beasts. It is here that the secret of our success lies.

It is being made in God's image then, that makes human beings special. This is true of each one of us, however limited our individual abilities may be. The unborn child is also made in that image.

> **Men and women have ordered the world to meet their needs because they are made in the image of God.**

The protection of God

The unique value of human beings is seen in the prohibitions against the taking of that human life wherein the image of God resides:

> Whoever sheds the blood of man,
> by man shall his blood be shed;
> for in the image of God
> has God made man.
>
> *Genesis 9:6*

The context of this prohibition is God's covenant with Noah. God has destroyed the peoples of the world through the flood because of their wickedness and is now re-establishing ground rules with Noah and his sons. God gives to them all the creatures of the earth for food, but they are not to take the lives of their fellow human beings.

This prohibition is made specific in the Ten Commandments with the sixth commandment stating simply:

> You shall not murder.
>
> *Exodus 20:13*

The supreme value of human beings is seen in the incarnate Son of God himself. He came to earth, to suffer death upon the cross in order to restore to humanity the relationship with God the Father which had been lost at the Fall. The price of our sinfulness was the life of God incarnate. This confirms the ultimate value of human beings in their Creator's eyes.

As we consider the unborn child, therefore, we must recognise that here is a life over which God has pronounced a solemn decree of protection.

The righteousness of God

The unborn child, made and protected by God, has a moral standing before him. Made in God's image, we are aware that we nevertheless fall short of God's righteous character. This is the problem of sin that stains all human nature and in which all of us – including the unborn child – have a share. David confessed that this was true of himself even from the time of conception:

> Surely I have been a sinner from birth,
> sinful from the time my mother conceived me.
>
> *Psalm 51:5*

The beautifully formed being in the womb therefore shares the same moral status as the rest of us – she is sinful (Ps. 58:3). This is true even though she is innocent of any sinful acts (and we may therefore refer to her as 'innocent' in some of our discussions). She needs the Saviour, just as we all do.

The call of God

In spite of sin, God graciously acts to call those whom he has chosen to be specially his.

> And those he predestined, he also called; those he called, he also justified; those he justified, he also glorified.
>
> *Romans 8:30*

This verse indicates that God's choice, being eternal, precedes the start of life: therefore, from conception onwards, those whom God chooses are chosen. However, the unborn child may also receive the call of God and experience the work of God specifically related to that call in the womb.

The unborn child may receive the call of God.

Thus we saw on page 4 that John the Baptist was filled with the Holy Spirit from his mother's womb, and began his work of witness three months before he was born (Luke 1:15,41).

Jeremiah describes his call to the prophetic ministry as occurring while he was still in the womb:

> The word of the Lord came to me, saying,
> 'Before I formed you in the womb I knew you,
> before you were born I set you apart;
> I appointed you as a prophet to the nations.'
>
> *Jeremiah 1:4–5*

The apostle Paul similarly speaks of his calling as being 'from my mother's womb' (Gal. 1:15) – a fact that is lost in some versions that translate this phrase as 'from birth'.

Samson's calling as a judge of Israel included being bound by a special vow to God. This vow was binding on him even as an unborn child (Judges 13:7).

Christ himself, whose special work is portrayed in the later chapters of Isaiah as that of the Suffering Servant, was formed by God in the womb with this work in view. Thus the Lord is:

> . . . he who formed me in the womb to be his servant
> to bring Jacob back to him
> and gather Israel to himself.
>
> *Isaiah 49:5*

And the call to that work came before birth:

> Before I was born the Lord called me;
> from my birth he has made mention of my name.
>
> *Isaiah 49:1*

The Son of God

The life of Jesus sheds the most revealing light on the spiritual standing of our child developing so amazingly in the womb. The essence of the Incarnation is that Jesus shared our human nature in every respect except one – our sinfulness (Hebrews 4:15). By assuming his human nature in the womb Jesus hallowed the first nine months of life. As we sing in the well known Christmas carol: 'Lo, he abhorred not the virgin's womb'.

Jesus did not bypass the early stages of human life.

God sent Jesus to earth as a zygote, embryo, fetus, child and man. He did not bypass the early stages of human life. He confirmed the continuity of human life from fertilisation to death. This means that we must treat unborn human life as holy, sacred and of the greatest value. For this reason Christians cannot consent to the destruction of human life by abortion because to do so would be to deny the truth of the Incarnation. It is no accident that many Christians celebrate the Annunciation. The life of the incarnate Son of God began with his conception by the Holy Spirit at that time. If there were no other reference to life before birth in Scripture this would be sufficient evidence for the value of the unborn child.

CHAPTER THREE

Arguments for abortion

*Woe to those who call evil good
and good evil,
who put darkness for light
and light for darkness.*
Isaiah 5:20

Every time an amendment to the law is mooted there is vigorous public debate on the rights and wrongs of abortion. Such debate is proper and essential since the issue is one of life and death; but, by the same token, discussion should be objective and informed. It is important to examine closely the most commonly heard arguments for abortion and to apply to each one the test of truth.

Medical and social arguments

Abortion concerns a woman's own body; she has a right to control her own fertility
Each pregnancy directly concerns two bodies (more, if it is a multiple pregnancy): those of mother and unborn baby (or babies). The weaker and more vulnerable – the baby – needs the mother's protection and nurture and relies on her love and goodwill for the very continuation of life. It is not the mother's body which is assailed with lethal intent in the abortion procedure, whether that involves dismemberment by suction or forceps, expulsion by drugs or intact surgical removal – though it is true that the mother may be accidentally damaged in the process. The very scientific tools which are so often used to detect disability with the aim of destroying the baby – ultrasound, fetoscopy, amniocentesis, etc. – also demonstrate the existence of a separate human being whose identity is physically and genetically distinct from the mother's, who may be of the opposite sex or a different blood group, or who may have a

It is not the mother's body which is assailed with lethal intent in the abortion procedure.

Facing page: A press and
poster campaign by SPUC
dealt with some of the main
arguments for abortion.

health condition quite at variance with her own. Since this
distinction exists from the start of unborn life – fertilisation –
the baby can never be regarded as part of the mother's body.

Correspondingly, since fertilisation marks the point at which
a new human individual comes into existence, great care must
be taken in discussing 'fertility control', which may be understood to mean contraception, sterilisation or abortion. While
there is a divergence of views among the churches on contraception and sterilisation (issues on which SPUC has no policy), it
must be noted that techniques which are truly contraceptive act
before fertilisation occurs; abortion, however, ends a human
life which has already begun. There is a crucial difference
between controlling the reproductive cycle of the woman's own
body and destroying an unborn child (see pp. 82–5).

Abortion is a woman's right to choose

Christians feel a natural unease at the justification of an action
by the assertion of 'rights'. In Scripture we are often told our
duties, but it is the rights of others that we are to defend. Ethical
decisions are made on the grounds of our responsibility to love
God and our neighbour (Matt. 22:37–40) rather than on the
exercising of rights.

However, even if one grants that people may freely exercise
'rights', there is no general 'right to choose' to do whatever we
like. We may have the right to choose to do many things, to
drink tea or coffee, or vote for the political party of our
preference, but we do not have a right to choose to rob banks or
mug old ladies. Where does abortion come on this scale? If it
were merely the removal of a piece of tissue, akin to having a
tooth pulled, then there would be no objection. But it is not.
Every unborn child is an individual human being; abortion
cannot be just a matter of maternal choice because it affects that
other human being. It violates that child's right to life.

Moreover, it is a mistake to assume that feminism should
always be equated with abortion advocacy. Groups such as
Feminists Against Eugenics have opposed the idea that abortion
should be part of a women's rights 'package deal'. They point
out that no one group of individuals can legitimately claim
'rights' at the expense of another: throughout history such
claims have led to injustice.

*Every human being
possesses the same
basic rights.*

Instead of assuming an inevitable mother-versus-baby conflict, we should consider what rights are at stake in abortion.
Every human being possesses the same basic rights and foremost among these is the right to life itself, for on that all other
rights depend.

There's always a good reason for having an abortion.

"It's my life. If I want an abortion I should be allowed to have one."

"I've just reached a crucial point in my job. I don't want to stop now."

"I'm not married. I couldn't possibly cope with a baby."

"My children are almost grown up. I really don't want another baby now."

"I can't face the thought of those dirty nappies and teething again."

"It's simple. I just don't want a baby."

"You're going to have a baby."

We know those words can strike horror into the hearts of many women.

And that becoming pregnant can be an inconvenience to them.

But should an abortion be so easy to get that the inconvenience can be brushed away?

And with it the life of an unborn baby?

Since the Abortion Act of 1967 the number of abortions in Britain has grown to over 172,000 a year.

On average, that's one every 3 minutes.

As the law stands two doctors need to agree that a woman's 'mental or physical health is at risk,' if she is to get an abortion.

However, some doctors are openly in favour of 'easier' abortions.

And they can be very generous in their interpretation of 'risk to mental or physical health.'

But one thing is certain.

However inconvenient a pregnancy might be, many women would think twice about an abortion if they could see how quickly the baby develops inside them.

23 days from conception – even before most women are sure they're pregnant – the baby's heart is beating.

As early as one month, the baby has a head, with eyes, nose, mouth and brain.

As early as two months, the baby will grab an instrument placed in its palm, and after nine weeks it can suck its thumb.

As early as three months, the baby can kick legs and feet, it has its own fingerprints, and starts to 'breathe' through the umbilical cord.

It is already perfectly formed.

It already has its own personality.

By the time a baby is born it has been living for nine months.

And an abortion takes that life away.

We are not using such emotive phrases to accuse or upset women who have had, or are thinking of having, an abortion.

But because we believe that a great many people – men as much as women – are concerned at the casual acceptance of abortion.

And would like to see this trend reversed.

If you are one of them there is something you can do to help.

Send a little of your money so that we can continue our campaign to protect the unborn child.

To continue to educate the public, to rally support in Parliament, and eventually to get the law on abortion changed.

We hope you will consider this an important cause.

After all, there are thousands of good reasons for <u>not</u> having an abortion.

All those childless couples, for example, who would do anything to adopt the baby.

And give it the life it deserves.

THE SOCIETY FOR THE PROTECTION OF UNBORN CHILDREN.

I would like to support your campaign to protect the unborn child.

'I enclose a cheque/postal order payable to SPUC for £_____ or please debit my Access/Barclaycard/American Express. *(DELETE AS APPLICABLE)

Card no. _____ Signature_____

Name_____
(BLOCK CAPITALS PLEASE)

Address_____

Please send your donation to: The Society for the Protection of Unborn Children, 7 Tufton Street, Westminster, London SW1P 3QN. For further information telephone 01-222 5845.

Every child should be a wanted child

At first sight this seems compassionate and irrefutable – until it becomes apparent that the argument really revolves around the fate of allegedly 'unwanted' children, who are to be aborted. Destruction does not constitute compassion. Yet is there truly any child who is unwanted? Certainly an unwanted pregnancy does not necessarily mean an unwanted child. Many children enrich the lives of their parents and are greatly loved, although their conception was neither planned nor intended. The alternative of adoption should always be offered in counselling of a pregnant woman: there are specialist organisations, such as Parents for Children, which place young people with special needs. SPUC Handicap Division includes members who have fostered or adopted disabled children as well as those who have borne them.

Even if it were ethical to kill unwanted children in their mothers' wombs, the evidence indicates that such an approach would not reduce the number of unwanted children in society. In a study carried out at the University of Southern California Professor Edward Lenoski found that 91 per cent of battered children passing through their medical centre were the results of planned and wanted pregnancies.[1]

One of the arguments which was used to support the passage of the Abortion Act was that it would reduce child abuse by reducing the numbers of unwanted children being born. However all of the evidence suggests that child abuse has increased.

The only large-scale continuous survey of child abuse cases in England and Wales comes from the National Society for the Prevention of Cruelty to Children (NSPCC). The NSPCC managed the Child Protection Registers on behalf of various local authorities from 1973–90, covering approximately 10 per cent of the child population of England and Wales. As Table 3:1 shows, from 1977–90 the number of children entered on the registers increased by over three times from 1,000 to 3,364, and the rate of children under 15 entered on the registers increased by five and a half times from 0.62 per thousand children in the age range to 3.4 per thousand.[2]

The most detailed figures are those relating to the physical abuse of children, as in the early days of the registers this was the only category of abuse which was recognised, apart from failure to thrive. The rate of physical abuse of children under 15 entered on to NSPCC registers is shown in Figure 3:1.

Such figures would suggest that the onus of proof is now on those who support abortion to demonstrate that killing children before birth leads to greater respect for children after birth.

The onus of proof is now on those who support abortion to demonstrate that killing children before birth leads to greater respect for children after birth.

Table 3.1 Numbers and rates of children on NSPCC registers, 1977–90

	1977	1978	1979	1980	1981	1982	1983	1984	1985	1986	1987	1988	1989	1990
Total abused	723	749	711	815	898	783	834	907	1,255	1,682	1,658	1,779	2,135	1,864
Accidental injuries	3	6	6	8	13	7	3	1	1	1	2	2	0	0
'At risk' or 'grave concern'	274	317	360	293	278	288	278	209	335	461	647	891	1,457	1,500
Total registered	1,000	1,072	1,077	1,116	1,189	1,078	1,115	1,117	1,591	2,144	2,307	2,672	3,592	3,364
Rate per 1,000 under 15s	0.62	0.67	0.67	0.72	0.84	1.06	1.16	1.16	1.68	2.32	2.50	2.66	3.60	3.40

Source: *Trends in Child Abuse, 1977–1982*, NSPCC, 1984: *Child Abuse Trends in England and Wales 1983–1987*, NSPCC, 1989: *Child Abuse Trends in England and Wales 1988–1990*, NSPCC, 1992.

Figure 3.1 Rates of physical abuse, children under 15 entered on NSPCC registers, England and Wales 1975–90

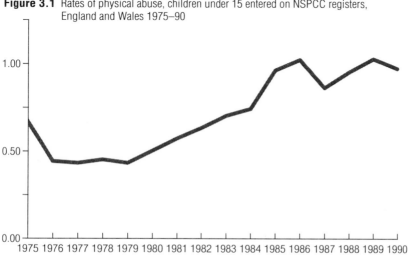

Source: NSPCC statistics

Ultimately, every child is wanted by God himself. He who clothes the grass of the field, feeds the birds of the air, and sees the meanest of them fall to the ground certainly has the most intimate concern for every child made in his image (Matt. 6:25–30; 10:29).

Ultimately, every child is wanted by God himself.

Back-street abortion would be a greater evil than a controlled legal situation

Pro-abortionists have always exaggerated the alleged incidence of back-street abortion. It is a common claim of pro-abortionists that before the 1967 Abortion Act was passed there were between 100,000 and 250,000 illegal abortions a year in Britain. However, a report of the Council of the Royal College of Obstetricians and Gynaecologists estimated that, based on hospital admissions and deaths, the number of criminal abortions taking place was in the region of 14,600:

Any other conclusion means that the results of criminal abortionists and of women interfering with themselves are better than those which can be produced by specialist gynaecologists terminating early pregnancies in the best hospital conditions.[3]

Pro-abortionists claim that the sharp drop in women dying following abortion (legal, illegal and spontaneous) is due to the passage of the Abortion Act 1967. However from 1967 to 1977 maternal abortion deaths in England and Wales fell from 32 to 6, a drop of 26 and this decline was no more dramatic than that in the decade preceding the Act, from 57 deaths in 1957 to 32 in 1967, a drop of 25.[4] These figures have been falling ever since records were kept and this is due to advances in medical care, not to the claimed impact of the 1967 Act. The official *Lane Report* noted a hundredfold drop in the maternal abortion deaths between 1936 and 1966, attributing this to the development of contraception and antibiotics.[5]

Furthermore the *Report on Confidential Enquiries into Maternal Deaths in England and Wales 1979–81*, showed that there were five maternal deaths following legal abortions and one following an illegal abortion during the three-year period. The pro-abortion media made much of the fact that the *Confidential Enquiries* for 1982–4 found *no deaths* from illegal abortion: the fact that seven deaths from *legal* abortions were noted was largely ignored.[6]

In the Republic of Ireland there were only two abortion deaths in the 10-year period 1979–88.

A certain amount of back-street abortion persists in Britain: from 1968 to 1988 police records show 986 offences of procuring illegal abortion and 293 prosecutions.[7] These facts, plus availability of abortion on demand, indicate that the situation is far from 'controlled'.

Conversely in the Republic of Ireland, where abortion has never been legalised and was in fact banned by a constitutional amendment of 1983, there were only two abortion deaths in the 10-year period 1979–88.[8]

In Portugal it was claimed in 1982 that illegal abortions caused the deaths of 2000 women a year.[9] However, according to World Health Organisation statistics, only 1887 women in their main childbearing years (15–44) died *from all causes* in Portugal in 1982.[10] Clearly, the 2000 figure was pure fantasy, plucked out of thin air.

We must regard abortion as a necessary evil until social problems (poor housing, overburdened mothers) have been overcome
To argue in this way is to grasp the wrong end of the stick.

ABORTION AND SLAVERY

The 'back street abortion' argument had an interesting parallel in the movement to abolish the slave trade. Those who supported slavery argued that, if Britain were to ban the trade unilaterally, it would simply be taken up by foreign competitors. In the words of one pamphleteer:

> If the trade should unfortunately be abolished . . . the immense profits . . . which result from it to England will be transferred to foreigners; your revenues will sink under the loss.[11]

By an ingenious twist, this argument was used to suggest that the slaves would be better off if the British stayed in the business. During a debate in the Council of Jamaica one slave-owner argued forcibly that the suppression of the slave trade by Britain alone 'would not promote the purposes of humanity' because slaves would become cheaper and the African chiefs would become 'more regardless for the lives of their captives'.[12] Furthermore, according to the captain of a slave ship, foreigners were capable of 'cruelty to the slaves, and a disregard of their comfort and even of their lives, to which Englishmen could never bring themselves to resort'.[13]

These arguments carried no weight with William Wilberforce, the great leader of the anti-slavery campaign. In a ringing speech to the House of Commons on 12 May 1789 he declared that the wickedness of the slave trade was so enormous, so dreadful and so irremediable as to admit of no solution short of its abolition. However powerful the arguments for its continuance might appear, justice demanded that it be stopped at once.[14]

The 'expediency' argument against abolishing slavery was wittily demolished by Sir

William Wilberforce (1759–1833) led the campaign against slavery. An unfinished portrait by Sir Thomas Lawrence (detail).

John Doyle MP, speaking in the House of Commons during the debate on the 1807 Bill which finally abolished the slave trade in Britain:

> Suppose a highwayman should urge as an excuse, that it is true he did rob the man, but it was because he knew that if he did not Will Bagshot's gang would, and that moreover it turned out a profitable job; and suppose that when pressed to relinquish so disgraceful an occupation, he should answer, 'but I have gone to great expense in purchasing horses, which would be fit for nothing else but the highway. I have built stables, but they will suit none but highwayman's horses, and I have purchased pistols and blunderbusses at great expense, which would be useless in any other calling'. I mention this merely to show how far the argument might be carried, and not as a comparison; for though no man has been more unhandsomely treated by highwaymen than myself, yet I would not degrade their profession by comparing it with the Slave Trade.[15]

Where there are problems of housing or poverty it is those which we should tackle: ending a baby's life achieves nothing positive for a mother in such a situation and may even add to her difficulties with possible physical or mental ill-effects of the operation (see Chapters 6 and 9). Availability of abortion may provide an excuse not to deal with social problems, particularly as the terms of the Human Fertilisation and Embryology Act 1990 permit abortion without time limit – i.e. up to birth – when a woman's actual or reasonably foreseeable environment is taken into account.

Although the 1967 Act was passed with reference to mothers worn out by continual childbearing, it is a fact that the majority of abortions are carried out on women who have no other children. Nevertheless it is essential to provide adequate levels of support for mothers in need. SPUC has pressed for extension of the maternity grant, urged the Maternity Services Committee to upgrade payments to disadvantaged mothers and campaigned successfully to secure the legal right to housing for homeless pregnant women. As Christians we must acknowledge our duty, not to kill, but to provide for those in need. This duty is expressed in the Old Testament's frequent concern for 'the stranger, and the fatherless, and the widow' – the vulnerable members of society whom God is seen to protect in a special way:

The majority of abortions are carried out on women who have no other children.

> The Lord watches over the alien
> and sustains the fatherless and the widow.
>
> *Psalm 146:9*

The world is overpopulated: without abortion it would be even worse

Sometimes people who find abortion repugnant, and who understand the development of life before birth, will still defend abortion as 'the lesser of two evils'. These people are so convinced that the 'population explosion' is bringing us to the verge of Armageddon that abortion becomes acceptable in their eyes as a means of slowing world population growth.

For the Christian the 'lesser of two evils' argument can never stand up because, if something is intrinsically evil and offends against God's law, we are not entitled to practise it on the understanding that some increase in social or economic well-being may result.

However, in a secular society there will be many who will adopt this approach. It is therefore important to make it clear that all serious research conducted into the effects of population growth in the last 25 years has gone against the 'population bomb' scenario.

Fear of population growth is not new. In the second century AD Tertullian wrote: 'Our numbers are burdensome to the world, which can hardly support us'.[16] In the fourth century Jerome wrote: 'The world is already full, and the population too large for the soil'.[17]

In Jerome's day the global population would have been only a few hundred million. Now it is nearly six billion, and the world still is not full! Human habitations cover only about 1–2 per cent of the land surface, and if everyone in the world went to live in Texas it would create a super-city with a population density about the same as that of inner London, leaving the rest of the world empty.[18] Even in densely populated England the amount of land in urban use accounts for only 10.2 per cent of the land area.[19]

There is no connection between population growth and prosperity.

In spite of the common assumptions, there is no connection between population density or population growth and prosperity. In 1967 the Nobel Prize-winning economist Simon Kuznets studied the data from the rich countries for the last 100 years, and from the developing countries since the second world war, to find out if rapid population growth caused slower economic growth. He was surprised to find that this was not the case. In fact it is easier to argue that economic growth and population growth usually go hand in hand. Western Europe, America, Australia and Canada provided examples of this in the nineteenth century; Japan, Singapore, Taiwan and Hong Kong in the last half-century.

Even the President of the World Bank (an organisation long committed to population control) now admits that:

> The evidence is clear that economic growth rates in excess of population growth rates can be achieved and maintained by both developed and developing countries.[20]

Where economies are stagnant or shrinking the reasons almost always lie in unjust and corrupt political systems, not in the number of children women are having. For example, China's communist government needed a scapegoat for the country's abysmal economic record, which contrasted strongly with the economic 'miracles' of other Asian countries like Japan. It was easier to blame women for having too many children than it was to admit that communism guarantees permanent poverty and absence of economic growth. Although we have been bombarded by population control propagandists with images of teeming Chinese (a sophisticated update on the old 'yellow peril'), China is less than half as densely populated as the UK.

Another popular argument for population control has been the fear that famines would become increasingly common, as an expanding population would outstrip the earth's potential for producing food. This was not a new argument: it had been propounded in 1798 by Rev. Thomas Malthus in his *Essay on Population*. Malthus predicted that population would grow faster than the food supply until famines acted as a brake.

Food supplies have been able to keep well ahead of population growth.

Malthus was wrong about the relationship between the growth of the population and the increase in the food supply. Food supplies have been able to keep well ahead of population growth from his time to ours. There has been an enormous increase in world population since the second world war, from about 2.5 billion people in 1950 to nearly six billion today, and yet as Figure 3:2 shows, food production has grown even faster. There is *more food per head of population* in the world now than at any time in history. In Western Europe, one of the most densely populated parts of the globe, we have to spend millions of pounds bribing farmers *not to produce*, or else the market

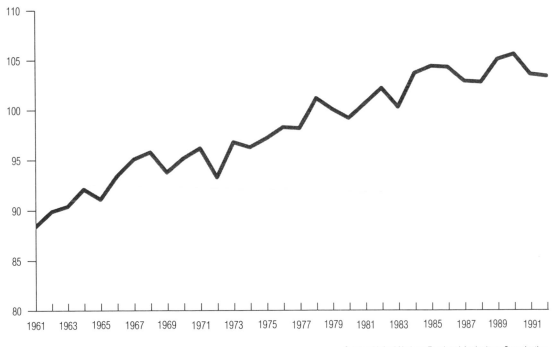

Figure 3.2 World food output per head of population 1961–92 (1979–81 = 100)

Source: United Nations Food and Agriculture Organisation

would be glutted. The fact that famines still occur in some countries is due to political factors, not to the inability to produce enough food.

How has this situation come about? In 1965 Ester Boserup, a Danish economist who had spent many years researching into agriculture for the United Nations, published her landmark study *The Conditions of Agricultural Growth*. In it she argued that advances in agriculture do not come about of their own accord, thus allowing population to grow, but rather that it is the other way round. It is the very *pressure of population growth* which forces communities to move from very easy but inefficient farming methods like forest fallow to more intensive methods like ploughing with livestock. As growing populations become more specialised and urbanised (in other words, people do not all live off the land) the farmers have a greater incentive to increase food production as they will have a larger market to sell into. Population growth is thus a good thing because it carries whole communities forward, from primitive to developed lifestyles:

> ... only in a densely populated region can a relatively efficient transport system exist without absorbing an inordinate share of the total labour force. Regular food transport to large towns is therefore possible only when relatively high population densities have been reached ... It thus appears that a population which is small in relation to the total territory it commands cannot, owing to this very smallness, get into a process of economic and cultural development.[21]

Although Ester Boserup's book was first published nearly 30 years ago, and the world's population has grown since then, her arguments still hold true. In 1992 the Overseas Development Institute published a study of the Machakos district of Kenya which revealed that, since the 1930s, the population has grown by more than five times, but agricultural output per hectare of land had increased by *more than ten times*:

Population growth is a good thing because it carries whole communities forward.

> Continuing population growth, in association with market developments, has generated new technologies which have supported both increased productivity and improved conservation of land and water resources.[22]

Other threats which were associated with population growth have been shown to be groundless. For example, there was a widespread fear, fuelled by books like *The Limits to Growth*,[23] that natural resources would be exhausted. Some people even drew up tables showing the dates by which certain resources would run out. Some of those dates have now passed and resources are more plentiful than they were before! In 1986 the prestigious US National Academy of Sciences published a study of the effects of population growth which stated that:

> There is little reason to be concerned about the rate at which population growth is depleting the stock of exhaustible resources . . . concern about the impact of rapid population growth on resource exhaustion has often been exaggerated.[24]

The more modern arguments for population control are based on the supposed link between population growth and environmental problems, but even here there is no conclusive evidence. A paper presented to one of the preparatory meetings of the 1992 United Nations Conference on the Environment and Development (the Earth Summit) by the Overseas Development Administration of the UK government admitted that:

> There is no single or simple general relationship between population and the environment . . . The danger posed by an over-active coalition between family planning advocates and environmental activists, at a time when the nature of the links between population and environment are still uncertain, is therefore real.[25]

Population growth can lead to improvements in the environment.

In fact evidence is now emerging to suggest that population growth can lead to improvements in the environment. The study of the Machakos district of Kenya referred to above reveals that environmental problems which worried observers in the 1940s, notably soil erosion, have been dealt with as a result of increasing manpower. Photographs of 'irreparable damage' from that period can be compared with photographs of healthy crops and trees on the same sites today.

At the extreme end of the Green movement we hear the argument that population must be reduced because *people themselves are a form of pollution on the planet*. This has led to the coining of the term 'popullution' or people pollution. This argument will have little appeal to Christians, however, as it is blasphemous. Men and women are made in the image and likeness of God (Genesis 1:26–27), and to treat them as though they were some noxious substance is to insult God himself.

Nor should we be swayed by arguments that human population growth means less space for animals and trees. The Bible leaves us in no doubt that man is not to be regarded as being on the same level with the rest of the creation. God made man to be with him for eternity. Man's needs are much more important than any supposed 'rights' of animals. As Arthur Kay has argued in *Calvinism Today*:

> ... the Bible repeatedly indicates that man's government (even that of the Canaanites) is to be preferred over that of the wild beasts (Exodus 23:28–29, Job 30:29, Isaiah 13:21, Jeremiah 50:39).[26]

'Man's government is to be preferred over that of the wild beasts.'

Christians who argue for population control find little support for their views in Scripture. God's instruction to Adam and Eve to be fruitful and multiply (Gen. 1:28) was repeated in his covenants with Noah (Gen. 9:7) and with Abraham (Gen. 17:6). Fertility and large families are constantly associated with God's blessing (Ps. 127:3–5; Gen. 22:17), while sterility is a misfortune or even a sign of God's disfavour (Hosea 9:11–14; 2 Samuel 6:23; Gen. 16:2).

Some people argue that these injunctions to be fruitful were given to God's people in a world less crowded than ours, and are no longer relevant. This implies that God lacked the foresight to see how his world would develop, and failed to make the temporary nature of his command explicit.

Arguments for population control which attempt to enlist biblical authority are unconvincing. For example, the author of an article entitled 'Unnumbered blessings' which appeared in the Christian magazine *Third Way* claimed that:

> Jesus gave up his chance of natural parenthood ... in order to give life to others ... remaining child-free is not necessarily a selfish choice.[27]

Many Christians would be made uneasy by this interpretation of the marital status of Jesus. It recalls the Christmas card produced by the Planned Parenthood Federation of America which depicted the Holy Family with the message 'God had only one Son – Follow HIS Example: Visit your local Planned Parenthood'.

Theological arguments
We turn now to some of the arguments which have particularly influenced the thinking of evangelical Christians on abortion.

The fetus does not have a soul
The discussion of 'ensoulment' – of when the human soul enters the body – has a long history. In the Middle Ages the Church

sometimes identified ensoulment as taking place *after* conception. The Greek philosopher Aristotle believed that the embryo was animated (gained a rational human soul) at 40 days in the case of a boy and 90 in the case of a girl. Animation was linked with an observable stage of fetal development, making a distinction between the formed and unformed child. The distinction found its way into the Septuagint 'translation' of Exodus 21:22–23 and hence (since the Septuagint was the Old Testament used by many early Christians), via Augustine's writings, into the complex law of the western Church.

This view of ensoulment did not lead the Church to conclude that abortion could be justified.

This view of ensoulment as a separate stage in human development after conception did not lead the Church to conclude that abortion could be justified. However, the fact that Christians have not always pointed uniquely to conception as the inaugural event of the human soul has been used in arguing for both abortion and embryo experimentation. Thus, the Archbishop of York referred to 'Christian beliefs about when the fetus should be treated as having full human value [differing] widely through the ages'[28] in defending experiments on human embryos up to 14 days old; and Mandy Coates, in a pamphlet that attempts to give a Christian justification to the National Abortion Campaign's fight for unrestricted abortion up to birth implies that because there have been different views on ensoulment, the Christian may take any view at all on the status of unborn children:

> It is quite possible to hold the view, as some Christians do, that the fetus only becomes ensouled when the woman carrying it decides to accept her pregnancy and continue with it until birth.[29]

The entire discussion of ensoulment as an event distinct from conception is based on a view of the soul inherited from the classical Greek philosophy of Plato and Aristotle. It is not informed by modern science and does not draw on the biblical view of man in which there is a unity of body and soul. It is therefore surprising that the idea of ensoulment enjoyed something of a revival among evangelicals in the early 1970s. This was due largely to the influence of *Abortion: the Personal Dilemma*, a book written by Rex Gardner, a gynaecologist and ordained minister. In it he advocated the view 'that while the fetus is to be cherished increasingly as it develops, we should regard its first breath at birth as the moment when God gives it not only life, but the offer of Life'.[30] This amounts to ensoulment at birth. Although Gardner has since changed his position[31] it is still encountered among evangelicals, particularly those who formed their views in the 1970s.

The biblical evidence for the ensoulment at birth view appears to be restricted to a single verse:

> And the Lord God formed man from the dust of the ground and breathed into his nostrils the breath of life, and man became a living being.
>
> *Genesis 2:7*

According to Gardner:

> This surely is the original biblical teaching that God took a fully-formed man and breathed into his nostrils the breath of life, and thus the man became a living creature – Adam.[32]

However, the analogy here is false. God's breathing of life into the first man is a unique event: it cannot form a pattern for subsequent repetition. In the Genesis account this is emphasised by the manner of Adam's creation: without human parents. It is not the birth of Adam that is described here; Adam had no mother to bear him. In the New Testament Paul shows that Adam stands as the representative of the whole human race (Rom. 5:12; 1 Cor. 15:21–22,49), just as Christ – whom he calls 'the last Adam' (quoting the Genesis verse: 1 Cor. 15:45) – is the representative of those whom he saves. We may therefore understand Genesis 2:7 as describing God's breathing of life not just into the man Adam, but into all mankind.

As we have noted, theories of ensoulment have tended to draw on an understanding of the soul found in Greek philosophy rather than in the Bible. In Scripture a human being is treated as a unity, rather than being divided into a separate body and soul. The soul is not so much a separate entity within human nature as a description of that nature. It is rather that we each are a soul, than that we have a soul. As Genesis 2:7 says: 'man became a living being' (or 'living soul' – AV). Gardner himself acknowledges this in his book, where he quotes James Barr:

In Scripture a human being is treated as a unity.

> The soul is not an entity with a separate nature from the flesh and possessing or capable of a life on its own. Rather it is the life animating the flesh. Soul and flesh do not therefore go separate ways, but the flesh expresses outwardly the life or soul . . . Man does not have a soul, he is a soul.[33]

Since the living body is present (whatever its stage of development) from conception onwards, we have no grounds for denying the presence of the soul.

The fetus is not a person

The moral implications of the biological fact that life begins at conception (see Chapter 2) are often evaded by arguments of this sort, which have gained wide acceptance in some evangelical circles. Perhaps the most influential of those who have followed this line of argument in recent years has been Gareth Jones, author of *Brave New People*.[34] The publication of this book in 1984 caused a major stir, particularly in the USA, but Professor Jones has defended and amplified his consideration of the 'personhood of the fetus' in his subsequent book, *Manufacturing Humans*.[35]

Quite rightly, Jones wishes to avoid identifying a stage (e.g. implantation or birth) before which an unborn child is a non-person and after which a person. However, he does this by use of 'the potentiality principle' which sees the:

> . . . human fetus [as] a potential person, in contradistinction to an actual person (a normal adult human being), or a being with a capacity for personhood (a temporarily unconscious person), or a possible person (a human sperm or ovum), or a future person (a person in a future generation).[36]

This designation of unborn children as 'potential persons' – a description that has become quite popular – is open to serious objections.

Beings that are not persons must be non-persons.

First, whatever else one might call them, beings that are not persons must be non-persons. Some people, of course, would be happy to call an unborn child a non-person, but those who pursue the 'potential person' line are usually keen to avoid this. Thus Jones asserts that 'at no stage is the embryo a non-person',[37] and that 'it would be wrong to conclude that this principle denies that the fetus is a "person"'.[38]

The attempt is being made here to place the unborn child into some sort of intermediate category between non-person and person. This is done by treating personhood as something that can be present in degrees; thus Jones uses terms such as 'increase in personhood', 'growth into personhood' and 'full personhood'. This is fair enough if by 'personhood' is meant the presence in a high degree of development of all the attributes and accomplishments belonging to persons; we may readily concede that, in this sense, the personhood of immature individuals is less than the personhood of mature, experienced individuals and might add that, taking this definition of personhood, even mature individuals display different degrees of personhood: we all know some whose life experiences and exceptional gifts make their personhood particularly full. This definition of personhood would also allow us to make sense of Jones's designation of a temporarily unconscious person as 'a being with a capacity for personhood'.[39]

However, if we consider 'personhood' to mean 'the state of being a person' we must ask whether it makes any sense to think of it as present in degrees. Can we really put two beings side by side and say that they are both persons to some extent, but that this one is more of a person than that one? We can hardly speak of 'half a person', as Jones concedes;[40] a person can only be one person, no more and no less. Personhood in the sense of 'the state of being a person' admits of no degrees.

We can hardly speak of 'half a person'.

It is this latter meaning of 'personhood' that is relevant to the discussion of the personhood of unborn children. For we are interested in issues of protection – whether we may forbid an abortion, or ban embryo experiments – and it is persons we are urged to protect. The question therefore is whether or not we have a person to protect. The confusion of the two meanings of 'personhood' gives the impression that we can have a being which is neither a person nor a non-person.[41] This is wrong; a being that is not a person is a non-person.

Second, the designation of unborn children as 'potential persons' should logically be extended to later stages of life. Certainly development continues in human beings for many years, and in some ways we could nearly always be said to have potential which we have not yet realised. How are we ever to identify a stage when we can say that by now the potential has definitely become actual? Jones states that 'the potentiality principle . . . only applies to *prenatal* existence',[42] but this restriction appears to be arbitrary. Though many who advocate the 'potential person' argument would wish to be generous in their assessment of the unborn child's personhood, it must be pointed out that others could give good reason for a very different assessment. Once the 'potential person' principle is admitted, the enormous amount of development still needed in unborn children must tell heavily against them. Even infants and toddlers have much potential unrealised, and this principle therefore undermines their protection as well. Jones cites Michael Tooley, who uses the categories of 'potential person' and 'quasi-person' in his justification of the killing of children up to three months after birth (potential persons) and possibly up to one year (quasi-persons).[43]

It is difficult to see a logical limit to the 'potentiality principle'. In theory we could all be classed as 'potential persons', with all that implies.

Third, we must ask what grounds can be offered for the protection of 'potential persons'. The very expression suggests that this will depend on what they may become, rather than what they already are. This is confirmed when the working of the 'potentiality principle' is formally enunciated:

> If, in the normal course of its development, a being will acquire a person's claim to life, then by virtue of that fact it already has some claim to life.[44]

But how is such a claim to be evaluated, especially when set against other claims belonging to those recognised as 'actual persons'? This question becomes acute when it is recognised that a 'potential person' is in fact a non-person (see above). If one kills a non-person, whatever the future might have held for it, it is still only a non-person one is killing. Given that even human spermatozoa and eggs may be considered potential persons, but are destroyed at will, one sees the logic of those who would allow the destruction of embryo, fetus or even neonate on similar grounds.[45]

More fundamentally, we must ask whether the basic distinction on which all arguments of this type rest can be justified. The distinction being made is that between being a person and being a human being (for the fact that biological life begins at conception is not denied). This distinction underlies all arguments that question the personhood of unborn children, whether by outright denial of personhood or by the subtle and cautious questioning exemplified in Professor Jones's work.

What do we mean by 'person'? In Scripture the term is most often used as a translation of the Greek or Hebrew words for 'face' (*prosōpon* and *panim* respectively), especially when 'face' stands for the outward appearance of a human being. There is, however, no development in Scripture of the concept of a 'person' as distinct from (or additional to) a human being.[46] The observation of Gareth Jones that 'no biblical passage speaks of humans possessing personhood before birth'[47] is therefore meaningless, for the Bible knows no distinction between humans and human persons.

What Scripture does teach us is the distinctiveness of human beings as against all other creatures. This distinctiveness consists in our being made in God's image (Gen. 1:26–27) so that we may represent him and live in relationship with him. Given

What Scripture does teach us is the distinctiveness of human beings as against all other creatures.

the personal nature of God himself,[48] it would not be unreasonable to summarise this distinctiveness by saying that human beings are persons – but this is doing no more than saying that they are made in his image. In biblical teaching the whole of humanity is made in this image; no human being can be excepted from this. Scripture therefore does not allow any human being to be considered a non-person: sex, race, age or stage of development can make no difference here.

Indeed, the Bible does treat human beings as possessing dignity and enjoying God's love irrespective of these categories. We must emphasise that unborn children are included here, and such passages as Psalm 139 and Jeremiah 1:4–5 (see pp.7–8, 25) clearly show that God's concern for human beings in this category is as great as for those in any other. Because all human beings are made in God's image he treats them in a special way. There is an obligation on us all to do the same and to treat other humans with respect for the same reason (Gen. 9:6). We may speak of this as our duty to respect or protect 'persons', but that must not be taken to mean that there are human beings whom we do not need to protect because they are 'non-persons'.

Because all human beings are made in God's image, he treats them in a special way.

Once a differentiation is accepted between human beings who are persons and those who are not, a dangerous path is opened up and that could lead almost anywhere. Who, then, is a person? Do we look for the ability to produce brain activity, or to recognise the presence of others, or to speak, or to pass a basic intelligence test, or to produce an Aryan pedigree? Once this distinction is allowed, personhood inevitably becomes defined in terms of achievement; it becomes something to be accomplished. The criteria for deciding who has attained the required qualities must necessarily be arbitrary and subject to opinion and change. We are placed in the position of deciding for ourselves who is and who is not a person; a frightening prospect.

The history of those who have designated some humans as 'non-persons' is a grim one. In the USA the 1973 *Roe v. Wade* decision of the Supreme Court that unborn children do not have the legal status of 'persons' was similar to its 1857 decision in the Dred Scott case that black slaves were not legal 'persons'. In Germany in the Nazi era the treatment of non-Aryans as effectively subhuman was given legal sanction when the Supreme Court there denied legal personhood to Jews in 1936.

The Christian view, hitherto generally accepted, is that we have a commitment to treat every human being as one of 'us' – as a 'person'.[49] We must love our neighbour as ourselves.

CHAPTER FOUR

The
hard cases

And we know that in all things God works for the good of those who love
him, who have been called according to his purpose.
Romans 8:28

Even among Christians who share the pro-life ethic, there exists an emotional pull towards allowing exceptions for the so-called 'hard cases'. Pregnancies which threaten the life of the mother, together with those resulting from rape or incest, represent the nightmare scenario for most people.

However, the scriptural and biological evidence that we have presented should lead us to the conclusion that the baby, however conceived, is an innocent human being in his or her own right. As Christians we know that it is people who sin: God does not make mistakes. He shows his goodness and care to us, whoever we are, and in spite of the sin which mars our lives:

It is people who sin: God does not make mistakes.

> The Lord is good to all;
> he has compassion on all he has made.
> *Psalm 145:9*

In the light of this, can we possibly justify the killing of an innocent baby, even in appalling circumstances, because of the crimes of others? Can we not rather trust the God who in all things 'works for the good of those who love him' (Rom. 8:28)?

Unfortunately, even among Christians, protection for the baby can be seen as less important than supposed compassion for the mother. And worse, in an abortion culture, abortion in these cases is increasingly seen as the *only* option, which narrows what the expectant mother sees as the range of choices open to her.

Before we examine these emotional and medical aspects, let us look at the factual and legal sides of these questions. It must be realised that pregnancy resulting from rape or incest is extremely rare, and abortion to save the life of the mother practically unknown today. Even adding in the abortion of handicapped babies, 98 per cent of all abortions are not for serious medical indications but for social reasons.[1]

Abortion and the life of the mother

There is probably no more potent argument for legal abortion than the case in which the continuation of the pregnancy puts the life of the mother at risk. As every pro-life campaigner will know, even the mildest attempt to restrict abortion will be met with objections of 'But you must have it to save the life of the mother', as if these cases constituted a significant proportion of the total.

In fact, they are almost non-existent. Out of 3,736,054 abortions carried out in Great Britain from the passage of the 1967 Abortion Act to the end of 1991 only 153, or 0.004 per cent, were carried out in an emergency for the stated reason of saving the life of the mother.[2]

However, the fact that the abortionist states that he has carried out the abortion to save the life of the mother does not prove that she would have died without the abortion. In 1982 the *Irish Medical Journal* published an investigation into the 21 deaths which had occurred among the 74,317 pregnant women treated at the National Maternity Hospital in Dublin between 1970–79. The authors of the study found that there was *not one single case* where an abortion would have saved the mother's life. They discussed in great length the details of the death of one woman who had severe congenital heart disease (Eisenmenger's Syndrome). All doctors would agree that this condition is life-threatening and pro-abortion doctors would certainly have no hesitation in advising an abortion on health grounds. Yet the authors of this study found that the published medical evidence showed that this condition carries a 30 per cent mortality in pregnancy (in other words, 70 per cent of pregnant women survived the delivery of their babies), and there was no evidence that abortion would be any less risky than childbirth. During the ten years covered by the study two other women who had Eisenmenger's Syndrome gave birth safely to three babies.[3]

Abortion and cancer

Very rarely a woman may have cancer and be pregnant at the same time. It is commonly argued that an abortion must be carried out in order to allow treatment of the cancer, as the cancer drugs would cause disability in the unborn. However, according to cancer specialist Professor James Fennelly:

There is no evidence that pregnancy makes cancer worse.

. . . there is no evidence that pregnancy makes cancer worse. There is no evidence that termination of pregnancy makes cancer better.[4]

In Professor Fennelly's experience, treatment can be given to the pregnant woman under specialised management which does not involve aborting the pregnancy.

There is the possibility that either the cancer or the treatment may cause a miscarriage or lead to an underweight baby, but this is very different from carrying out a direct abortion.

Abortion and ectopic pregnancies

Fertilisation takes place when the man's sperm meets the woman's ovum in the fallopian tubes. The fallopian tubes extend, one on either side, from the upper part of the womb to the ovaries. After fertilisation the embryo makes its way down the fallopian tube and into the womb where it implants itself in the lining, ready to grow. However it sometimes occurs that the woman's fallopian tubes become partially blocked, allowing the sperm through, but not open enough to let the embryo (which is many times larger) pass into the womb. In these cases the newly-created being begins to develop *in the fallopian tube itself*. This is called an ectopic pregnancy. As the tube is not capable of expanding, like the womb, to accommodate the growing child, it soon reaches a point, around six weeks after conception, when the tube ruptures. In these circumstances emergency surgery becomes necessary as the woman's life is in danger.

Sometimes a doctor may detect the presence of an ectopic tubal pregnancy prior to rupture, and in that case there is no doubt that the affected part of the tube must be removed. In the present state of medical science it is impossible to save the life of the baby in such a case. He will die whether the tube is removed or not. If the tube is not removed, the baby will die when the tube ruptures – and the mother's life will also be at risk. If the tube is removed, the baby dies as a result, but the mother's life is saved. The latter course is chosen to save the one life that can be saved.

The removal of a tubal ectopic pregnancy is not generally regarded as an abortion procedure since the *primary* intention is to protect the mother's life, not to destroy her unborn child.

Unfortunately there has been a rapid increase in ectopic pregnancies in recent years. This is thought to be because there has been an increased rate of pelvic inflammatory disease (PID) which can lead to an ectopic pregnancy by scarring a woman's fallopian tubes. It is also believed that the use of the coil or IUCD as a means of fertility control (see pp.83–4) increases the number of ectopic pregnancies. According to birth control experts Vessey and Doll:

There has been a rapid increase in ectopic pregnancies in recent years.

> . . . unplanned pregnancies occurring in women using an intrauterine device are much more likely to be ectopic or to end in spontaneous abortion than usual and there is some evidence that such abortions are particularly likely to be septic, occasionally with fatal results for the mother.[5]

Rape as a campaigning issue

From a purely legal point of view, if there were a law which allowed abortion only in cases of rape, it would be virtually impossible to establish or deny any claim that a pregnancy resulted from rape or incest. *For this reason, British law does not even mention rape as grounds for abortion.*

Arguments for legalised abortion based on these criteria are extremely dangerous because, while they seem to limit abortion to small numbers of very 'hard cases', they effectively legalise abortion on demand. Hence the appeal of the rape argument to pro-abortion campaigners.

Roe v. Wade

In the USA, prior to 1973, abortion was a matter for state legislation, rather than federal legislation. The availability of abortion varied from one state to another, with very liberal provisions in New York and California and very limited availability in most of the rest of the USA. However the test case which came before the American Supreme Court in 1973 of *Roe v. Wade* changed the situation completely, resulting in a ruling that abortion must be available to all women as a constitutional right.

Roe v. Wade was always assumed to have been based on a rape case. This was the argument presented in court and (just as important) in the overwhelmingly pro-abortion media. Although the court ruling did not actually mention rape as the factor which had swayed the judges' opinions, it was inconceivable that they had not been affected by the highly emotive nature of the discussion which surrounded the case of a young woman supposedly made pregnant by force.

In September 1987 Americans learned that *Roe v. Wade* was a fabrication.

The story told by Jane Roe, real name Norma McCorvey, was tragic. The young waitress had claimed that she was gang-raped in an assault by three men and a woman when she was working with a circus touring in Georgia. Pregnant as a result, she did not qualify for an abortion in her home state of Texas, which decreed that a mother's life had to be in danger to justify an abortion, and she was too poor to afford the fare to travel to California where abortion for rape was legal.

The case had all the right emotional ingredients to present her as an innocent victim of the law, and two pro-abortion lawyers pursued the case for four years until the Supreme Court handed down its notorious ruling which legalised abortion on demand in the USA. Since then over thirty million American babies have been killed by abortion. When voices began to be raised about the scale of abortion in the USA since 1973, the case of Jane Roe was raised as a banner for the 'Right to Choose'.

The lie was discovered during a television interview in 1987 when Norma McCorvey admitted:

> I found I was pregnant through what I thought was love. I was too poor to leave Texas for another state where abortion was legal. By claiming I was gang-raped I thought I might get an exception from the Texas law.

She did not.

> I was very depressed. I felt 'How dare they tell me that I couldn't abort a baby I didn't want'. I was very, very bitter.[6]

The law was fashioned in response to the false claims of an angry and distressed woman.

The Supreme Court had been swayed by this fabricated story. The law was fashioned in response to the false claims of an angry and distressed woman.

Norma McCorvey, unable to have an abortion, had a baby girl who was adopted, and whom she never saw again. One of the great ironies of this case is that it has since been reported that her daughter has been involved in pro-life activities, grateful that she is alive, and working to save other unborn babies.

The British experience

In England it was an actual rape case in 1938 that brought about a significant change in public attitudes to abortion and in the interpretation of the Offences Against the Person Act, which outlawed abortion. A 14-year-old girl who had been gang-raped by soldiers was aborted by gynaecologist Aleck Bourne, who then gave himself up to the police. He was tried and acquitted on the grounds that he had acted to safeguard the girl's mental health (see pp.62–3).

It was on this verdict that British abortion law was based until the passing of the 1967 Abortion Act. For many years doctors used their judgement in 'hard cases', but it became so loosely interpreted that, prior to the 1967 Act, any woman who threatened suicide could obtain an abortion in some parts of Britain. The prohibition on abortion was so seriously weakened by the verdict on this 'hard case' that it eventually led to the Abortion Act (1967) and the introduction of abortion on demand into Britain, in spite of all assurances that this would not be the result (see p.64).

Any woman who threatened suicide could obtain an abortion in some parts of Britain.

The assault on Ireland

At the beginning of the 1980s Ireland and Belgium were the only Western European countries still to afford legal protection to unborn children. However, it became obvious that a campaign was under way to legalise abortion in Ireland, and that the campaign was a carbon copy of that which had already been waged so effectively in Britain.

The 1861 Offences Against the Person Act was still in effect in Ireland (having been passed when Ireland was part of the UK) and this outlawed abortion. However, all that is needed to revoke a law is the passage of another law. It became obvious that the only way to keep abortion out of Ireland would be an amendment to the Constitution guaranteeing the right to life of the unborn. This could not be overridden, except by another referendum.

The referendum took place on 7 September 1983. Voters approved by 66 per cent to 33 per cent the following wording:

> *Article 40.3.3*
> The state acknowledges the right to life of the unborn and, with due regard to the equal right to life of the mother, guarantees in its laws to respect, and, as far as practicable, by its laws to defend and vindicate that right.

The strength of support for the unqualified protection of unborn children surprised many, including those who wished to see abortion introduced into Ireland. It was obvious that the chance of finding a majority to vote in another referendum in favour of abortion was extremely remote. The pro-abortionists would have to devise other tactics. True to form, they went looking for a test case.[7]

The rape of the amendment

In January 1992 the parents of a 14-year-old girl in Dublin discovered that their daughter was pregnant. She claimed to have been sexually abused since before her 13th birthday by the father of a schoolfriend. The parents decided to bring the girl (Miss X) to England for an abortion, but before leaving they asked the police to send an officer with them to obtain fetal material from the aborted baby which could be subject to DNA testing to identify the father. The police contacted the Director of Public Prosecutions who in turn contacted the Attorney General to see if such evidence would be admissible in court. On 5 February the police informed the parents that the evidence would be inadmissible. In the course of the conversation, the parents stated that they would be leaving for England the next day for the abortion.

On 7 February the Attorney General obtained an *ex parte* injunction in the High Court restraining the parents from arranging an abortion until the case could be brought before the High Court on 10 February. The parents were contacted and returned to Dublin with Miss X still pregnant.

The case was heard on 10 and 11 February, and judgement was delivered on 17 February restraining the defendants from interfering with the right to life of the unborn and restraining Miss X from leaving the jurisdiction for nine months.

The parents appealed to the Supreme Court where, on 26 February, the judges set aside the injunction of the High Court, permitting Miss X to travel to London for her abortion. In their ruling, delivered on 5 March, the judges found by a 4–1 majority that Miss X was entitled to an abortion, in Ireland if needs be, on the basis that her right to life was endangered by the continuation of the pregnancy *by virtue of the fact that she had threatened to commit suicide if she could not have the abortion*. They therefore regarded the abortion as justifiable under the terms of the pro-life amendment to the Constitution which recognised the 'equal right to life of the mother'.

The only medical evidence presented to the Court had been that of a clinical psychologist who had seen the girl for one consultation. As Mr Justice Hederman pointed out in his dissenting judgement, a clinical psychologist is not a medical practitioner. Furthermore no mention was made of evidence which indicates that suicide is so rare among pregnant women that pregnancy seems to act as a *protective* against suicide. A pregnant woman is up to twenty times less likely to commit suicide than a non-pregnant woman of the same age. Moreover, it has been shown that if a woman really is suicidal during

Pregnancy seems to act as a protective against suicide.

The Miss X case in Ireland became the basis of a bitterly-fought campaign to repeal the constitutional ban on abortion in the Republic.

pregnancy, she is more likely to respond to proper psychiatric treatment than to an abortion, which increases her depression and also carries the risk of severe post-abortion psychosis.[8]

However, the effect of the Supreme Court ruling was to make abortion available in Ireland, since any woman could say she was suicidal if it enabled her to obtain one. Furthermore there would be no time-limit on abortions in such circumstances as the woman could make such a claim at any stage of pregnancy.

The media coverage of the Miss X case had been so intense and so widespread that it reached to Africa and Latin America. Ireland was depicted as a barbaric country, stuck in the Middle Ages, refusing even to allow its citizens freedom of movement. In fact, although much had been made of the 'right to travel' issue, Irish women had been travelling to England for abortions since the passage of the 1967 Act. Out of approximately 35,000 Irish women who have travelled to England for abortions since the 1983 referendum, only one was issued with an injunction by the Attorney General – Miss X! The Attorney General claimed that he had no discretion in the matter once it had been drawn to his attention, but in May 1992 a man from Derry reported to the police that his girlfriend was planning to travel to Britain for an abortion. No action was taken.

Moreover, although the case was referred to in the media as 'the Irish rape case', the man accused was not charged with rape but with unlawful carnal knowledge, as the girl was under the age of consent (i.e. 17 in Ireland) and there was no claim that violence had been used. The relationship appeared to have continued over several months. This is not what most people understand by pregnancy resulting from rape.

The accused was not charged with rape but with unlawful carnal knowledge.

The legacy of Miss X

The Supreme Court ruling left the Irish people shocked and stunned: they thought they had voted decisively to keep abortion out of Ireland in 1983, only to have the words of the amendment to the Constitution twisted to reverse their intentions.

Furthermore, it had become clear that the old pro-abortion lobby had regrouped around the Miss X case (although there was no evidence to suggest that either Miss X or her parents had any involvement with it). Whereas in 1983 those campaigning against the pro-life amendment to the Constitution had claimed that they were not pro-abortion, they just did not think the amendment was necessary, now some of those same people were openly pro-abortion. It was clear that they were not interested in abortion for limited 'hard cases' like raped school-girls: they wanted abortion on demand and there was a grave danger that the ruling in the Miss X case would give it to them. The only answer seemed to be another referendum which would make it quite clear to the Government and the courts that the killing of Irish babies was not acceptable to the people.

The Government agreed that another referendum was required. However, on 6 October 1992 it was announced that there would be not one but *three* referendums, dealing separately with the right to travel to another country to have an abortion, the right to receive information on the availability of abortion in other countries, and what was called the 'substantive' issue of whether abortion should be permitted in Ireland under certain circumstances.

There were objections to the wording on the 'substantive' issue as it only allowed people to say whether or not they believed the Constitution should be amended to permit abortion on certain limited grounds, excluding suicide threats. It did not allow people to vote for no abortion at all, because a vote against the amendment was a vote for the *status quo*, and the Supreme Court judges had already interpreted the Constitution as allowing abortion for threats of suicide.

On 5 November the Irish Parliament was dissolved and a

General Election was called for 25 November. It was also announced that the three referendums on abortion would be held *on the same day*. In spite of the difficulties of campaigning in such a short time span, the pro-life movement in Ireland was rewarded with a strong vote *against* the substantive motion to introduce abortion in certain circumstances. (It was acknowledged that those who voted 'no' on the substantive motion were in fact voting against any sort of legalised abortion in Ireland). The motions for the right to receive information on abortion and travel to have abortions were carried.

There was little doubt in anyone's mind that the Miss X case had been used to further the pro-abortion agenda in Ireland.

The individual and the 'hard case'

The fact that 'hard case' arguments have been used to introduce abortion on demand does not alter the fact that, for the women who constitute the 'hard cases', the situations they face are agonising. Women who are pregnant through rape or incest are probably less interested in legal and constitutional consequences than they are in their own particular and distressing circumstances. So how should the Christian respond to demands for abortion in these terrible conditions?

Abortion and rape

Many would return the violence of killing an innocent baby for the violence of rape. But before we make that decision we should realise that most of the trauma has already occurred. Rape has already taken place; nothing will make it go away. That trauma will stay with the woman all her life.

'The victim's problems stem more from the trauma of rape than from the pregnancy itself.'

In the majority of cases, the pregnant victim's problems stem more from the trauma of rape than from the pregnancy itself.[9]

Will abortion help the pregnant woman or will it in fact bring her more harm? Contrary to what we might expect, post-abortion trauma in many rape cases appears to be no less pronounced than post-abortion trauma in non-rape cases.[9] Rape followed by pregnancy followed by abortion leaves a trail of three traumatic assaults: the woman is traumatised initially by the rape; the unborn child is destroyed by the abortion; and the woman is traumatised a second time by the abortion.

Will she be able to live comfortably with the memory that she killed her developing baby? Or will she ultimately be more at peace with herself if she knows that, even though she became pregnant in the most appalling of circumstances, she neverthe-

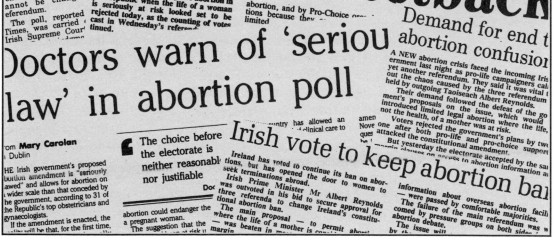

Pro-life group demands new abortion poll after 'no' vote

From **Mary Carolan**
in Dublin

AS the results from most of the Republic's 41 constituencies last night showed a comprehensive 2-1 defeat for the government-sponsored amendment providing for limited abortion, the Pro-Life Campaign issued a demand for a new abortion poll.

The PLC and the Society for the Protection of the Unborn Child claimed the clear rejection of the amendment indicated the electorate's total opposition to the introduction of abortion.

However, pro-choice groups hailed the result as a victory for their campaign against the amendment and urged the incoming government to introduce laws...

Yesterday's results demonstrated a clear rejection — in some constituencies as high as 80 per cent — of the main amendment providing for abortion in circumstances where there was a real threat ... mother's life.

On the basis of the count most constituencies, the amendment has been defeated to 34 per cent.

The other two amendment the rights to travel and to abo information, have been pa although by smaller majorities t the opinion polls had indicated, ticularly in relation to the information amendment.

The final result on travel was pected to be 66 per cent 'yes' ar 34 per cent 'no'.

Support for abortion amendments drops as archbishop gives the thumbs down

From **Mary Carolan**
in Dublin

SUPPORT for the three abortion amendments has fallen after the Archbishop of Dublin said he would be voting No to them next week.

An opinion poll carried out on Friday after Archbishop Desmond Connell spoke out and published in the *Sunday Independent* yesterday revealed the margins in favour of all three amendments had dropped.

On the main abortion amendment ... provides for abortion ...

ments still command the suppor large majorities.

Two out of three voters intend vote Yes to the travel amendme while just 23 per cent say they w vote No and 11 per cent a undecided.

On abortion information, 68 p cent intend to vote Yes; 21 per cen No and 11 per cent do not know

Such large margins indicate the latter two amendments will be comfortably carried. The main abortion amendment is also likely to be endorsed.

However, statements from prominent Catholic clergy are having an ... O'Connell's views were ...

Majority votes no, yes, yes in referendums

THE Government-sponsored stitutional amendment provi limited abortion in the Rep pears to have been reje large section of the electorate.

A majority seems to to the substantive am ther two.

Dublin governme plans abortion la

By **MICHAEL DEVINE**

ABORTION emerged as a serious issue today in the Republic's general election campaign as the Government published proposals for legislation which it intends to bring in if its constitutional amendment on abortion is defeated in next Wednesday's referenda.

Three referenda on abortion are being held on the same day as the general election.

The Government has urged the electorate to vote "yes" to the three proposals: to allow Pregnancy termination where the life of a woman is seriously threatened; to allow information to be provided on abortion facilities available abroad ... women to ...

O'Connell, confirmed toda tion in less restricted circum be legislated for if the constitutional amendment "substantive" issue of ab defeated.

He said the Government up a panel of consultants in a hospitals who would be empov direct that abortion should tak if a real and substantial threat life of a woman existed.

The Labour Party immed attacked this latest proposal on tion by the Government.

The Pro-Life Campaign, which backing a number of indepen candidates in the election, said it outrageous that the G ...

Reynolds opposes abortion referendum

... opinion poll today showed ... ar support for changing ... land's constitutional ... rtion but Prime ... bert Reynolds ca ... ongly against a refer ...

A total of 66% supporter ... amending the ban, a e Market Research Bu nd survey, and 55% w onwide vote on the is annot be changed referendum.

The poll, reported Times, was carried Irish Supreme Cour ...

The court's five judges are to detail their reasons this week and Mr Reynolds said a full Cabinet statemen ... nolds ... made then.

... ion of a refer ... the ...

Abortion setback

THE PROPOSAL to legalise abortion in the Republic when the life of a woman is seriously at risk looked set to be rejected today, as the counting of votes cast in Wednesday's referend ... tinued.

abortion, and by Pro-Choice or ... tions because they ... limited

Demand for end t abortion confusion

A NEW abortion crisis faced the incoming Iris ernment last night as pro-life campaigners cal yet another referendum. They said it was vital t out the chaos caused by the three referendum held by outgoing Taoiseach Albert Reynolds

Their demand followed the defeat of the go ment's proposals on the issue, which would introduced limited legal abortion where the life, not the health, of a mother was at risk.

Voters rejected the government's plans by two one after both pro-life and pro-choice support attacked the constitutional amendment.

But yesterday the electorate accepted by the sai ... clauses on access to abortion information an

Doctors warn of 'seriou law' in abortion poll

From **Mary Carolan**
in Dublin

THE Irish government's proposed ... bortion amendment is "seriously ... awed" and allows for abortion on ... wider scale than that conceded by ... he government, according to 31 of ... he Republic's top obstetricians and gynaecologists.

If the amendment is enacted, the ... ... will be that, for the first time, ...

❝ The choice before the electorate is neither reasonabl nor justifiable

abortion could endanger the a pregnant woman.

The suggestion that the ...

... untry has allowed an ... clinical care to

Irish vote to keep abortion ba

Ireland has voted to continue its ban on abortions, but has opened the door to women to seek terminations abroad.

Irish Prime Minister Mr Albert Reynolds was outvoted in his bid to secure approval for three referenda to change Ireland's constitutional abortion ban.

The main proposal — to permit abortion where the life of a mother is ... was beaten in m ... margin

amen Nove ques he l

information about overseas abortion facili were passed by comfortable majorities.

The failure of the main referendum was w comed by pressure groups on both sides abortion debate.

The issue will by th ...

less solved her problem by being completely unselfish, by giving of herself and her love to an innocent baby, who had not asked to be created, by allowing him to be born, and then later, if she felt it were in her baby's best interests, allowing the child to be put forward for adoption?

This may also demand great love and understanding by her husband or boyfriend or parents, who may have to struggle to accept the circumstances of such a conception:

> As to what factors make it most difficult to continue her pregnancy, the opinions, attitudes, and beliefs of others were most frequently cited; in other words, how her loved ones treated her.[10]

If we kill the baby by abortion, it certainly does not help the baby. It *may*, in the very short term, relieve the mother of an immediate burden, but this may have as much to do with helping those around her who may be unable to cope with her rape pregnancy. The long-term memory of the child that once was, no matter what the circumstances of his or her conception, will stay with her. As John Powell says, 'Yesterday's experiences are today's memories'.[11]

'Yesterday's experiences are today's memories.'

Alternatively, the mother is given all the support and assistance that counselling and loving concern can offer. She is helped to new heights of courage and respect for human life. The baby is allowed to live, and is possibly offered for adoption. This mother's experiences of today leave her with tomorrow's memories of her courageous and generous commitment to life.

Compare this memory with the woman who can only look back and say 'I killed my baby'. It is true that the child is the rapist's child but it is also true that it is her child. If a woman (and those around her who love and care for her) can somehow reclaim the violence and make the child their own, they and she can to some extent diminish the 'power' of the rapist. Ultimately, children should not be punished for crimes committed by their fathers.

In their book *Abortion: Questions and Answers*, Dr and Mrs Willke recount these two stories:

> In her beautiful autobiography, *His Eye Is on the Sparrow*, Ethel Waters reveals that she was conceived following the rape of her 13-year-old mother, at a time when rape treatment was unavailable. Her mother's love and Ethel Waters' value to society were not diminished by the circumstances surrounding her conception.

They go on to relate that a woman called them after they had answered questions on rape on a radio show and said:

> You were talking about me. You see, I am the product of rape. An intruder forced his way into my parents' house, tied up my father and, with him watching, raped my mother. I was conceived that night. Everyone advised an abortion. The local doctors and hospital were willing. My father, however, said, 'Even though not mine, that is a child and I will not allow it to be killed!' I don't know how many times that, as I lay secure in the loving arms of my husband, I have thanked God for my wonderful Christian father.[12]

Abortion and incest

Pregnancy as a result of incest presents similar questions to rape, but still the innocent victims remain the mother and her unborn child. According to George Maloof, writing in *The Psychological Aspects of Abortion*:

> As socially inappropriate as incest and incestuous pregnancies are, their harmful effects depend largely on reaction of others to the discovery of the incest.[13]

The victim of incest is usually very young, and at the mercy of a family trying to hide what is going on. The male perpetrator obviously is not a well-balanced person and, unfortunately, the mother often knows what is going on even if she will not consciously admit it. Abortion on a young girl in these situations may have serious physical consequences for her, particularly if the pregnancy is not discovered or acknowledged until a late period of gestation. Very often the girl is totally confused about her feelings for 'daddy', hating the sexual assault but still loving the father or the father figure at other times.

Abortion may actually prolong incest abuse.

Abortion may actually prolong incest abuse. A case was reported in Eugene, Oregon in 1990 when a mother and father were given two jail sentences for incest on their three daughters. Over a period of some years, there had been ten abortions on the three girls. The incest only came to light when the mother took one of the girls back to the same clinic instead of going to a new one as she had done before. The judge made the point that if the first pregnancy of the first daughter to be abused had come to light, the two other daughters would have been spared the abuse, and the first girl would have been exposed to less abuse. Abortion actually allowed the abuse of incest to continue.

The need to stand firm

Whatever we may think about abortion in cases of rape and incest, one thing is clear: the percentage of abortions resulting from rape and incest – where a woman has no control over her body – is miniscule compared with abortions resulting from pregnancies which have occurred to women who did have control over their bodies.

Nevertheless, the acceptance of abortion as a legitimate response to pregnancies which result from rape or incest makes it all the more difficult to oppose abortion for other pressing reasons (see pp.62–5):

> From the gut-wrenching cases of rape and incest, to the 'hard-ship cases' where abortion is done under empathetic circumstances, to purely selfish 'abortions of convenience', all the many reasons given for killing unborn children ultimately fail. It's *life* that is interfering with our lives. *Life* that is being 'gotten rid of.' *Human life* that we are killing in the name of difficult circumstances and bad timing.[14]

Difficult circumstances and bad timing should enable us to throw ourselves before the throne of our heavenly Father.

Difficult circumstances and bad timing should enable us to throw ourselves before the throne of our heavenly Father, asking for his love and protection, whether for ourselves or for others. This is what he has promised us. He has pledged that he will not leave us or forsake us. Do we not trust him who created us in love, and created every human life that comes into being?

CHAPTER FIVE

Abortion
and the law

Righteousness exalts a nation,
but sin is a disgrace to any people.
Proverbs 14:34

It is a common misconception that the legal prohibition of abortion is a recent phenomenon. In fact the unborn child has enjoyed the protection of the law since ancient times.

The unborn child has enjoyed the protection of the law since ancient times.

The first recorded law on abortion was in Sumeria in the eighteenth century BC; punishments were recorded for causing an abortion both deliberately and accidentally. The Babylonians have also left a record from the sixteenth century BC of the punishment for causing an abortion, as did Tiglath Pileser, King of Middle Assyria, whom we know of from the Old Testament (2 Kings 16).

From common law to statute
Under English law abortion has always been a crime. A textbook of the law written around the year 1250 by Henry de Bracton, one of Henry III's judges, stated that abortion was a type of homicide.[1] Throughout the centuries it continued to be a crime under common law and in 1803 a statute known as Lord Ellenborough's Act made abortion a felony punishable by death.

The Offences Against the Person Act of 1837 established the law substantially in its modern form. It was re-enacted with slight alterations in 1861, making abortion a felony punishable by a maximum sentence of penal servitude for life.

It was an oddity of English law that while it was murder to kill a person who had been born, and a felony to kill a child in the womb, there was no statute to cover the destruction of a child while in the process of being born. To fill this gap the Infant Life (Preservation) Act 1929 created the offence of child destruction, whereby it became an offence to 'destroy the life of a child capable of being born alive' by any wilful act which 'causes a child to die before it has an existence independent of its mother' (Section 1.1).

This Act did not only cover the period of birth: it had implications for the child in the womb as well, because it applied to any time before the child had 'an existence independent of its mother'. Its protection extended to any unborn child 'capable of being born alive'. Obviously this state is reached long before delivery, and the Act stipulated that evidence of 28 weeks of pregnancy was *prima facie* proof that this stage had been reached. The mention of 28 weeks was intended to save time and expense in proving what would be obvious in most cases; it was *not* intended as an indication that no child of shorter gestation could survive.

The only exception allowed under the Infant Life (Preservation) Act was an abortion carried out in good faith to preserve the life of the mother. This was always described as 'induced birth' and doctors were compelled to do everything possible to save the life of the child as well as the woman.

Rex v. Bourne

These two pieces of legislation made all abortion illegal in England.

The conjunction of these two pieces of legislation – the Offences Against the Person Act 1861 and the Infant Life (Preservation) Act 1929 – made all abortion illegal in England and additionally made the destruction of any unborn child which was 'capable of being born alive' illegal unless such destruction was done only for the purpose of preserving the mother's life. However, a test case provoked by gynaecologist Aleck Bourne in 1938 broadened the grounds under which an abortion could be carried out legally.

Bourne decided to abort a 14-year-old girl who had been raped by several soldiers. He was charged with carrying out an illegal abortion contrary to section 58 of the Offences Against the Person Act 1861. The case became a *cause célèbre (Rex v. Bourne* [1939] 1 KB 687) and turned on Bourne's justification of his plea of not guilty on the grounds that he felt the girl's mental health would have been adversely affected by giving birth.

Bourne was acquitted after a controversial summing up by Mr Justice Macnaghten who stated, without any authority, that the proviso permitting an abortion to save the life of the mother, which had been included in the 1929 Act, should be read back into the 1861 Act, and that in his view there was no essential difference between risk to the mother's life and damage to her health. He stated that an abortion would be lawful if carried out to prevent the woman from becoming 'a physical or mental wreck'.

The effect of the Bourne case was to open the stopcocks which eventually led to the collapse of the dam. Abortion came to be regarded as acceptable if it was carried out to prevent damage to the physical or mental health of the woman. As the grounds for abortions of this type became more and more liberally interpreted by some practitioners, Bourne became alarmed by what he had done. He complained that:

> Mr Justice Macnaghten, in his summing up, included the word *mental* 'wreck' as justifying the operation. This gave a wide latitude to phoney psychiatrists for giving certificates, as second opinions, on a plea of mental disturbance due to an unwanted pregnancy, especially in the unmarried . . . The common threats of suicide, which I have so often heard, are usually a form of blackmail.[2]

'The common threats of suicide are usually a form of blackmail.'

Bourne's view has been confirmed by recent research which shows pregnancy to be *protective* against suicide. That is to say, a pregnant woman is *much less likely* to commit suicide than a non-pregnant woman of the same age.[3]

Aleck Bourne, a courageous man, became more and more appalled by the results of his case. He was totally opposed to the Abortion Act which he predicted would lead to 'the greatest holocaust in history'. He became a founder member of the Society for the Protection of Unborn Children, and remained a member of the Executive Committee until his death.

Abortion law reform

Although the number of abortions which were performed for supposed serious medical reasons increased after the Bourne case, abortion was certainly not widely available on demand. Those who wished to see the law liberalised campaigned vigorously in Parliament for a change in the law to legalise abortion, and several unsuccessful attempts were made before David Steel introduced his Private Member's Bill to reform the abortion law in 1966.

Pro-abortion campaigners knew that Parliament would be unwilling to make abortion available on demand, or even to agree to any very substantial liberalisation of the law. David Steel's Bill was therefore presented in a minimalist or negative light: its supporters claimed that it would not make abortion easily available, it would only clarify the law, enabling doctors to abort in borderline or 'hard' cases without fear of prosecution.

Contrary to popular belief the Bill, which became the Abortion Act 1967, did not legalise abortion. *It did not replace the Offences Against the Person Act 1861 or the Infant Life (Preservation) Act 1929.* It merely stated that those carrying out an abortion would be exonerated from prosecution under those earlier Acts provided they complied with the conditions set out in the 1967 Act. The Act states, for example, that no one involved in an abortion would be guilty of an offence if the abortion were carried out by a doctor after two doctors had certified in good faith that one or more of the six grounds listed in Table 5:1 applied.

The Abortion Act 1967 did not legalise abortion.

David Steel and his supporters went to great lengths to persuade MPs and the public that it would not result in abortion on demand. During the House of Commons debate on his Bill David Steel claimed that ' . . . it is not the intention of the promoters of the Bill to leave a wide open door for abortion on request'.[4]

Much was made of the hard cases – the rape victims, the hard-pressed mothers of large families,[5] the cases in which the mother's life was at risk. The debate, which was taking place against the background of babies born with disabilities caused by thalidomide, was also heavily influenced by fear of handicap, and a wish to 'eliminate' it in the sense of destroying handicapped babies.

Opponents of the Bill argued that the wording of the grounds under which abortion could take place was so loose that it would lead to abortion on demand. In particular, Ground 2 seemed to allow abortion for a wide range of indications at the

Table 5:1 Grounds for an abortion as listed in Schedule 2 of the Abortion Regulations 1968

1 The continuance of the pregnancy would involve risk to the life of the pregnant woman greater than if the pregnancy were terminated;

2 The continuance of the pregnancy would involve risk of injury to the physical or mental health of the pregnant woman greater than if the pregnancy were terminated;

3 The continuance of the pregnancy would involve risk of injury to the physical or mental health of any existing child(ren) in the family of the pregnant woman greater than if the pregnancy were terminated;

4 There is a substantial risk that if the child were born it would suffer from such physical or mental abnormalities as to be seriously handicapped;

or in an emergency:

5 To save the life of the pregnant woman; or

6 To prevent grave permanent injury to the physical or mental health of the pregnant woman.

Figure 5.1 Abortion by statutory grounds, England & Wales, 1981–89, as percentage of all grounds

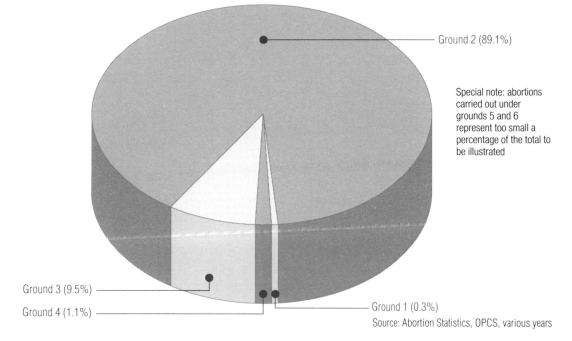

Ground 2 (89.1%)

Special note: abortions carried out under grounds 5 and 6 represent too small a percentage of the total to be illustrated

Ground 3 (9.5%)

Ground 4 (1.1%)

Ground 1 (0.3%)

Source: Abortion Statistics, OPCS, various years

doctor's discretion in a way which could lead to abortion being available virtually on demand.

The Abortion Act was passed in a half-empty House of Commons on Friday 14 July 1967 after an all-night sitting by 167 votes to 83. It received the Royal Assent on 27 October 1967 and came into force on 27 April 1968.

The abortion industry

It quickly became clear that the law had, in fact, given a mandate for abortion on demand. In 1969 – the first full year of the Act – there were 58,363 abortions carried out in Great Britain. In 1970 this rose to 91,819 and in 1971 to 133,110. The majority of abortions carried out under the Act cited Ground 2, which had indeed paved the way for social abortion, or abortion on demand (see Figure 5:1). It became obvious that any woman seeking an abortion could get one, either on the National Health Service or in the private sector. A Gallup Poll survey conducted in January 1988 among 746 gynaecologists (accounting for 40 per cent of all gynaecologists in Great Britain) revealed that 85 per cent said that they either had worked or were working in NHS hospitals where abortion on demand was practised. Only 11 per cent of respondents stated that they had never had such experience and 3 per cent said they did not know.[6]

The Abortion Act was passed in a half-empty House of Commons.

As private clinics were opened, staffed by doctors prepared to operate on anyone who could pay the fees, Britain – and particularly London – became the abortion capital of the world. Although the Soviet bloc had legalised abortion long before, Britain was the first western country after Sweden to do so.

Abortion tourism brought women from all over the world to make use of a law which, while it was claimed to be quite restrictive in its wording, was being given a very liberal interpretation. This, in its turn, increased the pressure on governments of other countries to liberalise their own laws to stop women from having to travel for the operation.

Many Commonwealth countries, which maintained close ties with Great Britain, soon realigned their laws on abortion to match ours. Other European countries liberalised their laws throughout the 1970s and 1980s. The example of the British law was used to promote the campaign for abortion in the USA where, in 1973, the US Supreme Court invalidated the abortion laws of all 50 states through its rulings in *Roe v. Wade* and *Doe v. Bolton* which legalised abortion on demand in the USA.

Abortion tourism to Britain fell off as a result, but the increasing numbers of resident women seeking abortions made sure that annual abortion totals continued to rise (see Figure 5:2).

Figure 5.2   Total abortions in England, Wales & Scotland, by year

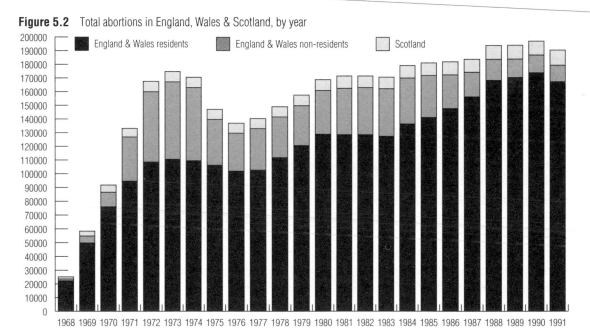

Comment: The 'peak' years of 1972–1974 contained record numbers of abortions performed on non-resident women in England & Wales. As these numbers declined the UK totals first declined then appeared to stabilise in the early 1980s. However abortions on resident women in England & Wales were steadily rising, and in 1984, the annual UK total exceeded the previous 'peak' of 1973.

Source: *Abortion Statistics*, OPCS, various years

An analysis of 21 years of abortion statistics carried out for the SPUC Educational Research Trust[7] revealed that the typical candidate for an abortion under the 1967 Act was young, single, childless and carrying a healthy baby – the very type of case for which MPs had been assured in 1967 that abortion would not be available. The 'hard cases' – the mothers of large families and women carrying handicapped babies – constituted a tiny fraction of all abortions.

Abortions carried out in an emergency to save the life of the mother – the most frequently cited of all the 'hard cases' in the abortion debate – amounted to 153 out of the 3,736,054 abortions carried out in Britain up to the end of 1991, or 0.004 per cent of the total. These abortions could have been carried out legally prior to the 1967 Act.

From the pro-life viewpoint 'hard cases' would not justify abortion (see Chapter 4). Human life is God's supreme gift, and as every human being has been designed by God to know him and love him in this world and the next, it is not up to us to designate any of our fellow human beings as 'unwanted'. Legalised abortion would be equally unjust if it were confined to 'hard cases'. However, we live in an increasingly utilitarian age in which many people are ready to make value judgements of their fellows based on materialistic assessments. It is this tendency which has been exploited by pro-abortionists to persuade the public and MPs to accept abortion legislation which was presented as restricted to 'hard cases', but which in reality could be given a liberal interpretation to allow abortion on demand.

It is not up to us to designate any of our fellow human beings as 'unwanted'.

The fightback

The Society for the Protection of Unborn Children was publicly launched at the House of Commons in January 1967 to oppose the passage of what was then called The Medical Termination of Pregnancy Bill. However this had already received its Second Reading in Parliament, and it proved too late to prevent it from passing into law as the Abortion Act 1967 on 27 October of that year.

SPUC has led the nationwide support for a number of parliamentary attempts to amend the Act and prevent abuses through the use of Private Members' Bills. Since James White's Abortion (Amendment) Bill 1975 these Bills have consistently won majorities, but they have not become law due to the delaying tactics of the pro-abortion minority. At the time of David Steel's Abortion Bill, Harold Wilson's Labour Government let it be known that all necessary time would be made available to facilitate the Bill's passage into law. The obstruction of debate by time-wasting procedural methods therefore became pointless, although pro-lifers forced two all-night sittings before Steel could get his Bill through. No such concessions were made for any pro-life attempts to amend the Act.

Life in a test tube

In the early 1980s the issue of the creation and use of human embryos was added to the pro-life agenda.

Louise Joy Brown, the first test-tube baby, had been born on 25 July 1978. It became clear that the manipulation of human embryonic material in laboratories raised the most serious ethical questions which were not covered by any legal framework. In 1982 the Government established a committee of enquiry under the chairmanship of Dame Mary Warnock, as she then was, to look into this question.

When the *Warnock Report* was published in 1984 it gave details of a range of practices involving not only the use of *in vitro* fertilisation (IVF) techniques designed to provide infertile couples with children, but also the creation and use of human embryos for research which could be of no possible benefit to the embryos themselves, which would ultimately be destroyed.

The *Warnock Report* recommended approval of virtually all of these practices,[8] including cross-species fertilisation (i.e. the use of human sperm and ova with those of animals) and the use of human embryos for experimentation up to 14 days after fertilisation.

It was obvious that such practices violated not only the individual's right to life, but also the age-old medical ethic that no procedures should be carried out on a patient which will not benefit the patient unless that patient has given a full consent to take part in experiments. Embryos used for testing drugs and for other purposes cannot give any such consent.

Embryos used for testing drugs and for other purposes cannot give consent.

In the 1984–5 session Enoch Powell MP introduced the Unborn Children (Protection) Bill to prevent the creation and storage of human embryos for any other purpose than implantation in a named woman – in other words, to stop the use of human beings as guinea pigs for experiments. The Bill was passed at Second Reading by a massive majority of 238 to 66 in February 1985, but failed for lack of time owing to a filibuster by pro-abortion MPs. Ken Hargreaves decided to re-introduce the Bill via the Ten Minute Rule procedure in 1986 to force a vote, in order to prove that a majority still existed for it. Although he won the vote, there was no parliamentary time available to debate the Bill. Similar Bills were later introduced by Alastair Burt (1986–7) and Ken Hind (1987–8) in the Commons and by the Duke of Norfolk (1989) in the House of Lords, but all failed for the same reason.

Government legislation

Although the Government had promised to introduce legislation based on the recommendations of the Warnock Committee, it was in no hurry to do so. It was unwilling to allocate precious parliamentary time to such a controversial issue, particularly when it looked as if the pro-life position would triumph! The promised legislation had to wait until the next Parliament, when The Human Fertilisation and Embryology Bill was introduced in November 1989.

Meanwhile there had been several attempts during the 1980s to amend the law by introducing time limits. As mentioned above, the Infant Life (Preservation) Act 1929, which was unaffected by the Abortion Act, made it illegal to destroy an unborn child who was 'capable of being born alive'. To the extent that this represented a time limit, it was the only time limit which the law recognised at that time, and it was well known that unborn children were often capable of being born alive and surviving as early as the 22nd week of pregnancy.

David Alton MP introduced his Abortion (Amendment) Bill in the 1987–8 session as a Private Member's Bill with the intention of making abortions illegal if carried out after the

A series of public meetings was held around the country to rally support for David Alton's attempt to restrict abortions.

18th week of pregnancy. After this and several other Private Members' Bills containing similar proposals were 'talked out' in the House of Commons by their opponents, the Government agreed to allow amendments to the Human Fertilisation and Embryology Bill – a Government Bill – which would permit MPs to vote on this issue.

Human guinea pigs

During the passage through Parliament of what became the Human Fertilisation and Embryology Act (1990) the Government was officially neutral on both time limits for abortion and the use of human embryos for research. However Kenneth Clarke, the Secretary of State for Health, and Virginia Bottomley, the Minister for Health, both supported the use of the human embryo for experimental purposes, as did Mrs Thatcher, the then Prime Minister.

The scientists involved in human embryo experimentation ran a campaign to persuade the public and MPs that, without access to human embryos, research into handicap would be impaired, and the use of *in vitro* fertilisation (IVF) would stop. The media collaborated enthusiastically, producing newspaper interviews and documentaries for radio and television in which the families of handicapped people spoke of their agonising problems which they believed could have been prevented by the sort of research on human embryos which some scientists wanted (see note 26, p.166).

A number of eminent scientists who opposed the use of human embryos for research found it almost impossible to have any input into the debate, as the media steadfastly ignored a viewpoint regarded by them as unhelpful.

Pro-life handicapped people also objected to the use of human embryos as guinea pigs on the grounds that, although they would have preferred not to have been handicapped, there are ethical boundaries which no research should transgress, however noble the aim. It was equally difficult for these people to make their voices heard.

Parliament eventually voted to allow the use of human embryos for experiments, including drug testing and the development of contraceptives. Indeed it had become increasingly clear from the way in which the pro-experimentation campaign had been waged that it was for these latter purposes that the pharmaceutical industry wanted the sanction of law. The enormous sums of money involved in contraceptive and abortifacient drugs and treatment make this a more appealing field of research than the cure of disability.

Eminent scientists who opposed the use of human embryos for research found it almost impossible to have any input into the debate.

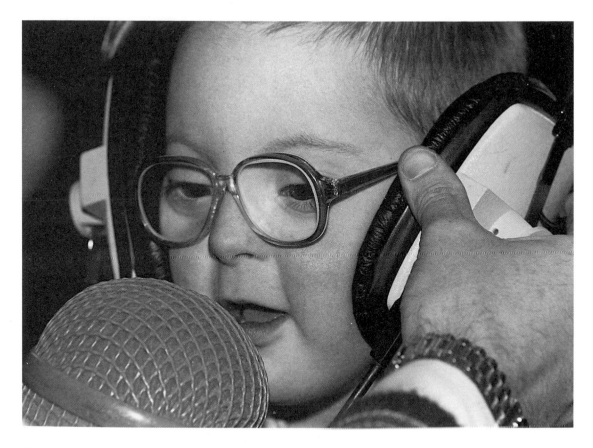

Time limited abortions

The attempt to introduce a time limit for abortions resulted in a further reduction in the degree of protection afforded by the law to unborn human life. Proposals to make abortion illegal after the 18th, 20th or 22nd week of pregnancy were defeated and Parliament eventually decided on 24 weeks. This so-called 'reduction' in the time limit was in fact an *increase* since the only 'time limit' previously existing was the one set by the Infant Life (Preservation) Act 1929, which stated that no unborn child might be killed who was 'capable of being born alive', and which took 28 weeks gestational age as *prima facie* proof of viability. Medical advances since 1929 had made much earlier babies viable. The protection which the Infant Life Preservation Act should have afforded them was now formally withdrawn.

The situation was made worse by the inclusion of exceptions to this 24-week rule to permit abortion at later stages of pregnancy wherever doctors believe that 'there is a substantial risk' that the child, if born, would be 'seriously handicapped' or that abortion is necessary to prevent 'grave permanent injury to

In spite of having Down's Syndrome, young John Broadbent was able to contribute to a pro-life press conference in the House of Commons.

Much of the debate surrounding the Human Fertilisation and Embryology Bill was based on the assumption that embryo research was needed to find treatments and cures for handicap. This was surprising, as the leading proponents of human embryo experimentation were quite open about their real aim, which was to eliminate handicapped people before birth. An interview with Robert Edwards in *The Times* had already made it clear that:

> The development of probes which identify specific genes in the embryo would allow couples with a family history of inherited disorders to have children by the test-tube technique. Any abnormal embryos could be excluded in the laboratory at a few days old, avoiding the risks and traumas of abortion four or five months into pregnancy.[9]

In a briefing paper from the President of the Royal College of Obstetricians and Gynaecologists, Professor M.C. Macnaughton, human embryos carrying sex-linked diseases were highlighted for the 'search-out-and-destroy' approach:

> It is very likely that it will be soon possible to sex the embryo at a very early stage. If the disease is only present in, for example, male offspring, then if the sex of the

embryo is male it would not be implanted.[10]

Therapeutic research on the embryo was not envisaged, just the exclusion of potentially affected embryos.

Even PROGRESS, the organisation formed to campaign for human embryo research, finally admitted that 'Research using human pre-embryos [*sic*] is not, and never has been, concerned with treatment of genetic disorders or chromosomal abnormalities'.[11]

At the same time, the public remained largely unaware that research into disability, and also into IVF, would have remained possible *without* the use of human embryos for experimentation. For example, Professor Jerome Lejeune, who discovered the extra chromosome 21 which is the cause of Down's Syndrome and is now researching into the treatment of the condition, has never felt the need to use human embryos in his work. Indeed, he wrote to *The Times* to explain that they would be useless for such research:

> Maturation of the blood, of the muscles or of the brain cannot be observed in human embryos of less than 14 days old. Hence troubles affecting these tissues must be studied in subjects having already developed the relevant organs.[12]

the physical or mental health of the pregnant woman' or that there is risk to her life. As no definition of 'seriously' or 'grave' is included in the 1990 Act, and as the doctors are permitted to take into account the pregnant woman's 'actual or reasonably foreseeable environment', it is clear that much is left to the doctors' discretion. Judging by past experience of interpretation of abortion law, these 'exceptional' cases will almost certainly become less exceptional than the MPs who voted for them imagined. The revised grounds for abortion are shown in Table 5:2.

Exceptional cases will almost certainly become less exceptional than the MPs who voted for them imagined.

This was the danger of which SPUC had been warning since the early 1980s, urging that MPs should not introduce an upper limit Bill since, sadly, a majority of MPs would demand exceptions which could lead to abortion up to birth.

Table 5:2   Grounds for an abortion under the 1967 Abortion Act as amended under section 37 of the Human Fertilisation and Embryology Act 1990

A The continuance of the pregnancy would involve risk to the life of the pregnant woman greater than if the pregnancy were terminated;

B The termination is necessary to prevent grave permanent injury to the physical or mental health of the pregnant woman;

C The continuance of the pregnancy would involve risk, greater than if the pregnancy were terminated, of injury to the physical or mental health of the pregnant woman;

D The continuance of the pregnancy would involve risk, greater than if the pregnancy were terminated, of injury to the physical or mental health of any existing child(ren) of the family of the pregnant woman;

E There is a substantial risk that if the child were born it would suffer from such physical or mental abnormalities as to be seriously handicapped;

or in an emergency

F To save the life of the pregnant woman; or

G To prevent grave permanent injury to the physical or mental health of the pregnant woman.

The 24-week time limit only applies to Grounds C and D. All other grounds are without time limit, i.e. up to birth.

This was, in fact, what happened, as Kenneth Clarke, then Secretary of State for Health, supported by Virginia Bottomley the Minister for Health, persuaded MPs to decouple the Abortion Act from the Infant Life (Preservation) Act 1929. Although this was presented as a bit of tidying up, it had the gravest consequences. The fact is that apart from the 24-week limit which had been included in the 1990 Act, there was no other time limit to check abortions carried out in any of the 'exceptional' cases mentioned above, apart from the 'time limit' imposed by the 1929 Act's prohibition on the killing of children 'capable of being born alive'. But once even that limited protection had been removed, it left a situation in which abortions could, in many cases, be carried out up to the time of birth. As a result, late abortions after 24 weeks have risen sharply. Such is the barbarity of current abortion legislation in England, Wales and Scotland.

Northern Ireland is in an exceptional position in that the 1861 Act still applies, as does the ruling in the case of *Rex v. Bourne*, but not the Abortion Act (1967) or its 1990 amendments as contained in the Human Fertilisation and Embryology Act, although the rest of that Act does apply there.

Opening Pandora's box

When the Abortion Act was being debated in 1967 its opponents warned that legalised abortion could open a Pandora's box of other problems, and that the taking away of respect for life in the womb would inevitably have a knock-on effect. These predictions proved to be tragically true.

The argument for abortion based on the 'elimination' of handicap – i.e. a seek-out-and-destroy policy in the womb – had always been one of the most popular justifications. Even those who are in many ways repulsed by abortion will say 'but you have to have it for handicap, of course'. This reaction is usually motivated by ignorance and fear of the unknown.

In the wake of the passing of the 1967 Act it became clear that doctors in some hospitals were increasingly unwilling to accept the birth of handicapped babies, who were seen as a challenge to their supreme medical skills. The development of sophisticated ante-natal tests and screening, which allowed for many babies with Down's Syndrome and other conditions to be 'got rid of', caused a certain resentment of the ones who got through the net. The handicapped newborn were regarded as damaged goods which, in a consumerist-orientated society, could be sent back to the maker.

The handicapped newborn were regarded as damaged goods which could be sent back to the maker.

It was well known that in some hospitals a regime was being followed to ensure that handicapped babies would not survive.[13] In 1981 a case came into court which tested the proposition that the law of Great Britain would allow for the deliberate destruction of the newborn handicapped along with the unborn.

Dr Leonard Arthur was charged with the murder of his patient John Pearson, a newborn baby with Down's Syndrome, but otherwise in good health. John Pearson was rejected by his parents but he needed no operation to survive and would have

lived, given ordinary care. However Dr Arthur put him on a course of 'treatment' which resulted in his death at the age of 3 days. He was given water only, not milk, and dosed with the drug DF118, which is not recommended for use with infants, in a dosage two and a half times that necessary to kill an adult male.

Even though the facts of the case were never in dispute, and the charge was reduced to manslaughter, Leonard Arthur was acquitted. He had been supported by many other physicians including Sir Douglas Black, President of the Royal College of Physicians, who took the view that in the case of 'a child suffering from Down's Syndrome and with a parental wish that it should nor survive, it is ethical to terminate life'.[14]

It was subsequently revealed that Leonard Arthur had operated a ruthless policy to destroy handicapped babies, with or without their parents' consent.

The verdict gave the green light to other doctors to practise infanticide of the newborn handicapped, which is now an

Ann Widdecombe MP joined SPUC supporters from Northern Ireland when they delivered 7,000 letters to the Prime Minister protesting against a proposed extension of the Abortion Act to Northern Ireland.

accepted part of medical practice in some hospitals.[15] It is the obvious outgrowth of legal abortion: if the handicapped can be hunted down in the womb up to the time of birth, why stop there? A few days more should be allowed to round up the stragglers in the opinion of some, including Francis Crick and James Watson, who received the Nobel Prize for their work on DNA. Watson suggested that the child should be on three days approval, and Crick favoured genetic screening to detect flaws. Any child who failed the test would forfeit the right to live.[16]

Euthanasia

When abortion and infanticide have been accepted by a society, euthanasia cannot be far behind. All of the same arguments can be used, in particular those based on the costs to society of supporting the 'useless' lives of those who, from a purely utilitarian perspective, are regarded as 'better off dead'. The notion of the 'life not worthy to be lived' is a flexible one.

The notion of the 'life not worthy to be lived' is a flexible one.

Thus far attempts to legalise euthanasia in the UK have failed. Even the permissive bodies which represent the interests of the medical profession have recommended against it, for the very simple reason that, once the sick or elderly patient has been despatched, no one knows if euthanasia was voluntary or not.

A number of cases of 'mercy killing' have come into court in which the prosecution has seemed reluctant, and the judge partial to the interests of the killers. We hear of the great 'compassion' and 'tender care', together with the 'great distress' which the killing caused the killer. Charges are dismissed, or else suspended sentences handed out. Effectively euthanasia is illegal, but you can do it and get away with it.

The 1993 ruling by the Law Lords in the case of Tony Bland, the 'Hillsborough Boy' who suffered injuries in a football stadium accident in 1989 and was described as being in a 'persistent vegetative state' (PVS), significantly advanced the campaign to legalise euthanasia, by permitting passive euthanasia (the deliberate killing of patients by withholding treatment). In the case of Tony Bland the provision of food and fluid by tube were for the first time defined as treatment so that he could be literally starved to death.

The facts of the case were as follows: Tony Bland's parents, together with his doctors and urged on by the Ethical Committee of the British Medical Association,[17] sought a judicial ruling that food and fluids could be defined as treatment, which would allow the hospital to stop feeding their son. There was nothing wrong with Tony Bland's digestive system, but his condition made it impossible for him to feed himself. The intention was that he should die of malnutrition/dehydration, in order to put an end to his persistent vegetative state. It is important to remember that although Tony Bland was severely handicapped and unable to communicate, he was not sick and he was certainly not dying. Indeed, his parents and doctors justified bringing the case by arguing that he might live for another twenty to thirty years.

The case went to the House of Lords where on 4 February 1993 the Law Lords ruled that the hospital would be justified in withholding treatment in the sense of starving Tony Bland. The argument had turned on whether or not the provision of food and fluids by tube can be regarded as treatment, since there would have been no need for a court case to establish that doctors need not continue to provide treatment to prolong the life of a person who is dying anyway. Food and fluids are a basic necessity of life and have not, until now, been regarded as medical treatment.

Food and fluids are a basic necessity of life and have not, until now, been regarded as medical treatment.

Tony Bland had never expressed any wish to have his life terminated if he ever fell into a dependent state. The decision was taken by his parents and doctors that his life was no longer worth living, a point recognised by Lord Mustill, one of the Law Lords: 'What is being said in this case is that he should be starved based on an assessment of his quality of life'.[18]

The Law Lords found that the hospital would be justified in withholding food, and Tony Bland died on 3 March 1993 of kidney failure which was a direct result of his being denied food and fluids.

The significance of the decision was not lost on Lord Goff, one of the Law Lords, who said that as the legislature (that is to say Parliament) was not prepared to grapple with the situation, the judiciary should act. The barrister acting for the hospital pointed out that this was what had happened in the Netherlands where doctors had been practising euthanasia for years on the strength of an agreement that they would not be prosecuted. Dutch law was actually formally changed in February 1993 to make the Netherlands the first country in the modern world, apart from Nazi Germany, to legalise euthanasia.

This precedent from the not-so-distant past should have alerted the Law Lords. The foundations for the Nazi extermination programme in the field of medical ethics were laid by a study conducted by Karl Binding and Alfred Hoche and published in 1920.[19] The study professionalised and medicalised the concept of destroying 'life unworthy of life', referring to this as 'purely a healing treatment'. It introduced the concepts of 'Ballastexistenzen' (human ballast) and 'empty shells of human being'. Putting such people to death 'is not to be equated with other types of killing . . . but [is] an allowable, useful act'.[20]

Nineteen years later, with the Nazi extermination programme in full swing, Dr Hermann Pfannmuller explained to a fellow psychiatrist that, 'We do not kill with poisons, injections etc . . . our method is much simpler'. This method consisted in a policy of slow starvation.[21]

The War Crimes Tribunal sentenced Dr Pfannmuller to six years' imprisonment, starting in 1949.

CHAPTER SIX

Abortion
and the doctors

*I have set before you life and death, blessings and curses. Now choose life, so
that you and your children may live.*
Deuteronomy 30:19

Methods of abortion currently used in Britain
We must now look at those methods of abortion which are
currently used in Great Britain.

Vacuum aspiration
This is the most commonly used technique, suitable for pregnancies of up to 12–14 weeks. The cervix (neck of the womb) is
dilated with instruments and a tube connected to a suction
pump applies negative pressure to the child, who is dismem-
bered. The pump works on the same principles as the vacuum
cleaner, but has ten times the force. Body parts are sucked into a
jar and checked to see whether abortion is complete. The
procedure is often terminated with curettage, or scraping out of
the womb, to remove any remaining fetal parts. Very early
pregnancies can be sucked out via a cannula, or tube, of only 6
or 8 mm diameter without using anaesthetic. This quick
outpatient procedure is sometimes described as a 'lunchtime
abortion'.

*Dilatation and curettage (D&C) and Dilatation and evacuation
(D&E)*
Both procedures are carried out under general anaesthetic on
pregnancies of up to 10 weeks (for D&C) or 20 weeks and even
more (for D&E) although the risk of complications rises after
16 weeks. The cervix (neck of the womb) is stretched open to
allow entry into the womb through the vagina. The abortionist
pulls or cuts the unborn child apart using either sponge forceps
or a curette (a metal or plastic instrument with a sharp loop at
the end). An instrument like a pair of pliers is needed for late
abortions, once the bones have calcified, as the skull must be

crushed and the spine snapped to facilitate removal.

Martin Haskell, an American abortionist who has performed an enormous number of D&E procedures, stated in a paper delivered to the National Abortion Federation Risk Management Seminar in Dallas on 13 September 1992 that:

> Most surgeons find dismemberment at 20 weeks and beyond to be difficult due to the toughness of fetal tissues at this stage of development.

He went on to outline his own technique of dilatation and extraction (D&X) which involved inserting scissors into the base of the baby's skull, opening the scissors, then inserting a suction catheter to evacuate the contents of the skull.

'Most surgeons find dismemberment at 20 weeks and beyond to be difficult.'

Prostaglandins
Prostaglandins (a class of hormone-like substances, now produced artificially) are administered to the pregnant woman by drip, into a vein in the woman's arm; by catheter, into the cavity of the womb adjacent to the sac in which the baby is lying; or by injections directly into the amniotic fluid in which the baby lives. After an interval of 12–24 hours they cause the womb to contract, delivering the baby prematurely. Using prostaglandins is now the most common method of late abortions. In the case of late abortions the baby will be large and fully formed, and the later the abortion the greater the risk of the baby's being born alive. Doctors may therefore inject urea or saline into the amniotic sac or potassium chloride into the baby to kill him before the abortion.

Hysterotomy
Abdominal 'Caesarian' surgery is performed under general anaesthetic and the unborn child is removed. The 'advantage' for medical scientists is that the child, who is intact and probably still alive, can be used for experiments. However the procedure carries a higher risk of mortality for the woman (mostly from embolism) and leaves a scar in the uterus which is liable to rupture in subsequent pregnancies. It is very rarely used now, unless the woman is being sterilised at the same time.

Hysterectomy
The womb is removed, complete with baby. Rarely used unless there is an associated uterine disease.

RU486: The abortion drug
In 1991 the Department of Health issued a licence for the use of

the drug RU486, making Britain only the second country in the world (after France, where it was developed) to license it.

RU486, also known as Mifepristone or Mifegyne, is a drug which can be used to procure medical abortions (as opposed to surgical abortions, which require an operation) up to nine weeks of pregnancy. It attacks the lining of the womb by interfering with the hormone necessary to maintain this lining, resulting in the expulsion of the baby. In order to make it effective it has to be used in conjunction with prostaglandins.

Because it functions as an abortifacient and not as a contraceptive it is covered by abortion law, and the standard forms have to be signed by two doctors. However, during the Report Stage of the Human Fertilisation and Embryology Bill in 1990 the then Secretary of State for Health, Kenneth Clarke, introduced an amendment to create a new 'class of place' in which abortions could be carried out. This was intended to facilitate the use of RU486 since, although it is currently only licensed for use in hospitals and clinics, it could also be administered in other places such as doctors' surgeries and family planning clinics.

Complications occur in 5–7.5 per cent of cases.[1] Up to 20 per cent of patients bleed for over 12 days; abortion may fail or be incomplete, leading to infection.[2] A consultant gynaecologist running trials of RU486 reported that theatre and blood transfusions would be necessary because of the problems of severe haemorrhage in some patients'.[3] One woman is known to have died and at least three others have suffered severe heart attacks in France. These are only the known short-term side effects. The procedure is still new and consequently nothing is known of long-term effects or the consequences of repeated use.

Abortifacient methods of fertility control

Many millions of women are using methods of birth control which, unbeknown to users, function by procuring early abortions.

Oral contraceptives
There are many varieties of oral contraceptives. The combined oestrogen/progestogen pill works primarily by suppressing ovulation. If no egg is released from the ovary, then the woman cannot become pregnant. However, it fails to do this in about 20 per cent of a woman's monthly cycles. In these cases it can also operate by making the mucus at the neck of the womb hostile to penetration by sperm. This effect is still *contraceptive*. However its third 'fail safe' mechanism is to alter the lining of

Many millions of women are using methods of birth control which function by procuring early abortions.

the womb so as to prevent implantation of the developing embryo should fertilisation have occurred. This effect is *abortifacient*. The progestogen-only pill, sometimes called the mini-pill, rarely suppresses ovulation and acts primarily by thickening the cervical mucus (the *contraceptive* effect) and by making the lining of the womb unreceptive to the developing embryo (the *abortifacient* effect).

Intra-uterine contraceptive device (IUCD or IUD) or coil
There are several types of coil and all require insertion into the uterine cavity. The presence of a coil within the womb does not prevent ovulation, nor does it prevent the man's sperm from fertilising the woman's ovum. Its mode of action is to stop the embryo from implanting in the lining of the womb once fertilisation has taken place. As Germaine Greer puts it:

> A device inserted into the uterus prevents intrauterine pregnancy, and intrauterine pregnancy only, by transforming the welcoming environment for the blastocyst into a toxic sink.[4]

However, birth control organisations which favour the use of the IUCD claim to be vague about the exact way in which it works, and insist on describing it as a contraceptive, because, according to Greer:

The abortionist was a disreputable figure on the fringes of medicine prior to the 1967 Act. Caricaturist George Cruickshank depicted her as a 'Brandy Ball' (far right).

. . . once the abortifacient action of IUDs was recognised in law they would become illegal in most countries, for however liberal the abortion laws, there are no legal codes which permit uncontrolled abortions to be carried out without the knowledge or consent of the woman, which is what happens in the case of IUDs.[5]

Post-coital contraception

If a woman has had intercourse without using any form of birth control, and she does not want to become pregnant, she can be prescribed the 'morning after pill'. This is a high-dose oestrogen oral contraceptive which must be taken within 72 hours of intercourse. It works by disturbing the lining of the womb to prevent the embryo from implanting. As with the two previous methods described, the embryo would be expelled from the womb. This constitutes *an early abortion*, and is not a form of contraception which (as the word suggests) works by preventing conception.

It is often a condition of prescribing the morning after pill that, if a woman fails to menstruate, she must agree to have an abortion because of the risk of damage to the unborn child, and the possibility of court action for compensation if a handicapped child were born.

Side-stepping the Abortion Act

The use of any methods of fertility control which work by unsettling the womb to prevent implantation of the fertilised ovum should be governed by the Abortion Act. It should be remembered that the Offences Against the Person Act 1861 is still on the statute book, and that sections 58 and 59 of this Act make it a criminal offence to 'procure a miscarriage' (i.e. carry out an abortion) unless the conditions laid down in the 1967 Abortion Act are met. It is clear that the contraceptive pill, the morning after pill and the coil must, on some occasions at least, work by procuring a 'miscarriage'. Furthermore, the provisions of the Offences Against the Person Act apply *even if the woman was not pregnant when the miscarriage was attempted*.

To bring these post-coital methods of fertility control within the scope of abortion legislation would prove a severe inconvenience to those who promote them, particularly the Department of Health. It would mean that they could only be prescribed by a registered doctor after two doctors had decided that one or more of the grounds for abortion had been met (see Tables 5:1 and 5:2).

The question has been side-stepped by redefining the meaning of miscarriage. In answer to a parliamentary question the Attorney General of the day stated that:

> The word 'miscarriage' is not apt to describe a failure to implant . . . the phrase 'procure a miscarriage' cannot be construed to include the prevention of implantation . . . Whatever the state of medical knowledge in the nineteenth century, the ordinary use of the word 'miscarriage' related to interference at a stage of pre-natal development later than implantation.[6]

As Dr John Finnis, Prelector of Jurisprudence of University College, Oxford, has shown, the Attorney General was wrong about the meaning of the word 'miscarriage' in the nineteenth century.[7] However, based on the Attorney General's statement, which was not supported by any medical, scientific or legal evidence, and which has never been tested in court, these abortifacient procedures are widely available, masquerading as 'contraceptives', without any regard to the restrictions contained in the Abortion Act.

After-effects of surgical abortion

A number of large-scale studies from around the world confirm that abortion carries the risk of serious consequences for the woman.

Early complications

A British survey of 6105 women having abortions found that 10 per cent returned to their doctors within 21 days suffering from complications. Of these complications 2.1 per cent were described as major, and 2.4 per cent were psychiatric.[8]

Abortion carries the risk of serious consequences for the woman.

A Danish study of 5,851 abortions carried out between 1980 and 1985 showed that 6.1 per cent of the women developed complications which required hospital admissions. The complication rate was highest in women under 25 and who were aborting a first pregnancy.[9]

Long-term complications

Having an abortion can significantly increase the risk of complications in subsequent wanted pregnancies. A study of 9,283 deliveries in America[10] between August 1977 and March 1980 showed that women who have had abortions are more likely to experience complications (see Table 6:1).

The effect of abortion on subsequent pregnancies is more severe in younger women. A Yugoslav study found the 14–16-year-olds who were pregnant after a previous abortion had a

Table 6.1 Complications of pregnancy, America, 1977–80

Complication of pregnancy	Number of previous abortions		
	nil	*1*	*2 or more*
Bleeding in first third of pregnancy	8%	10.7%	12%
Premature rupture of membranes	4.1%	4.2%	7.5%
Breech or other abnormal position of the baby	4.6%	5.3%	6.7%
Low birth weight (<2.5kg)	7.0%	7.2%	10.3%
Premature birth	6.6%	7.6%	9.5%

10.7 per cent rate of miscarriage, compared with 5.5 per cent of older adolescents with a previous abortion. Of the 14–16-year-olds who had had a previous abortion 24 per cent delivered premature babies, compared with 10.3 per cent of girls of the same age who had not had abortions.[11]

Post-abortion pelvic infection

The 'sexual revolution' of the 1960s has led to an explosion of sexually transmitted diseases.

The 'sexual revolution' of the 1960s has increased the incidence of frequent sexual activity with multiple partners. This has led to an explosion of sexually transmitted diseases, some of which are hard to detect and treat.

One of these, chlamydia, is increasingly common in women, infecting the neck of the womb. It is often symptomless, so women may be unaware for years that there is any problem.

However, the effect of the abortion is to carry the infection, via the abortionist's instruments, into the womb where the raw tissue and blood left behind by the abortion provide the ideal environment for the organism to flourish and spread infection to the fallopian tubes. The medical term used for this infection is pelvic inflammatory disease.

Various studies have shown that 10–40 per cent of women presenting for abortion have chlamydia infection, and of these 10–25 per cent will develop post-abortion pelvic infection.[12] In other words, between 1 and 10 per cent of all women having an abortion will be affected in this way. According to the *British Medical Journal*, pelvic inflammatory disease carries a 17 per cent chance of tubal infertility, a 20 per cent chance of chronic pelvic pain, a 40 per cent chance of deep dyspareunia (painful intercourse) and an 80 per cent chance of menstrual disturbance. There is also a sevenfold increase in the risk of ectopic pregnancy.[13]

Table 6.2 Admission to psychiatric hospital, Denmark, 1975

Age Groups	Aborting women	Delivering women	Other women
	(Rates per 10,000 women)		
<20 yrs	11.4	6.2	4.9
20–24	18.9	10.5	6.8
25–29	20.6	11.4	7.0
30–34	25.4	16.6	9.0
35–39	17.0	26.2	9.4
Total	18.4	12.0	7.5

Psychological complications

In Denmark during 1975 all admissions to psychiatric hospitals were monitored in order to compare women who had had an abortion within the previous three months with women who had given birth within the previous three months.[14] As Table 6:2 indicates, the differences were striking.

These findings have been confirmed by similar studies from other countries. A review article in the *British Journal of Psychiatry* found that approximately 10 per cent of women having an abortion will suffer marked, severe or persistent psychological or psychiatric disturbances.[15]

The world out of joint

It is clear that abortion is not the simple, safe procedure which many women have been led to believe it to be. Perhaps we should not be surprised, as it offers a violent intervention in the beautiful, delicate and miraculous sequence of events designed by God to allow men and women to bring new life into the world. Through bearing children we are allowed to become co-creators with the Almighty, not just of a physical entity like members of the animal kingdom, but of a new human being created in God's image and designed for eternal life with him.

To throw this gift back, to refuse to participate in the miracle of creation once it has begun, is an affront to the natural order, which was created by God himself. The fact that, even in the world's most technologically advanced societies, abortion appears to have unavoidable physical and psychological consequences is a witness to what happens when the world is put out of joint.

Abortion is not the simple, safe procedure which many women have been led to believe it to be.

CHAPTER SEVEN

Research on humans

My frame was not hidden from you
when I was made in the secret place.
Psalm 139:15

It was not until the late 1700s that the existence of mammalian egg and sperm cells, and the process of fertilisation, were discovered. This process remained beyond the control of doctors and scientists until, in the 1970s, the technique of *in vitro* fertilisation (IVF) was developed which allowed the human embryo to be created *outside the woman's body* in a laboratory.

This raised the most profound ethical questions which no society had previously had to face. What was the moral and legal status of these embryos? Who did they 'belong' to? Did they have rights? If not, was there anything wrong with using them as experimental material?

Of all the alarming developments of modern science, IVF brought us closest to the Brave New World.

Of all the alarming developments of modern science, IVF brought us closest to the Brave New World. Robert Edwards, the pioneer of test-tube babies along with Patrick Steptoe, recorded his excitement when he found that mouse eggs could be ripened *in vitro*:

> Surely the whole field then was within my grasp – cows, sheep, monkeys – and man, too, if I could only get their eggs?[1]

Soon he got the eggs. The first test-tube baby, Louise Brown, was born on 25 July 1978. However, the attraction of IVF procedures did not end with the provision of babies to infertile couples, as science correspondent William Breckon made clear:

> Ultimately we could have the know-how to breed these astronauts or dustmen, soldiers or senators, each with identical physical and mental characteristics most suited to do the job they have to do.[2]

Other scientists produced even more alarming statements of the sort which used to be associated with the Professor Branestawm characters in science fiction films:

> It would mean we could manipulate at will the genetic pool, produce super races, modify ethnic traits, excise socially unacceptable habits – in fact, produce people to order.[3]

Public concern grew as it became clear that there was no legal provision for the control of such work, as the situation was an entirely new one. Scientists were claiming that they could, and would, use human embryos for research work which could be of no value to the human – i.e. the embryo – concerned, since at the end of it the embryo would be destroyed, dissected or flattened on a glass slide.

It became clear that there was no legal provision for the control of such work.

It was in this atmosphere that the Government set up the Warnock Committee to investigate the whole area of IVF and embryo research, and to make recommendations for legislation.

Throughout the 1980s the debate was intense. Pro-lifers argued that the use of human beings, at any stage, for destructive research was unacceptable and breached the most fundamental ethical principles laid down in the Helsinki Declaration of the World Medical Association in 1964 (revised 1975):

> The doctor can combine medical research with professional care, the objective being the acquisition of new medical knowledge, only to the extent that medical research is justified by its potential diagnostic or therapeutic value for the patient . . . In research on man, the interest of science and society should never take precedence over considerations related to the well-being of the subject.

Destructive embryo research clearly goes outside these guidelines. It cannot benefit the patient – i.e. the embryo – nor can the embryo give consent like a patient who agrees to take part in trials of a new drug. However, the benefits which it was claimed would accrue from embryo research were, for many scientists, the apples of Hesperides, worth going to any lengths to obtain. Ethics would just have to catch up. Dr Peter Braude of the Fertilisation Unit of the Rose Maternity Hospital, Cambridge spoke for many of his colleagues when he said: 'The Helsinki agreement was drawn up long before embryo research began, and thinking has not yet caught up with it.'

The Helsinki Declaration was, however, drawn up after the Second World War with the specific intention of preventing a recurrence of the abuse of medical science under Nazism. Dr Braude might have done well to remember the words of another doctor who chafed against the restrictions of a much earlier statement of medical ethics, the Hippocratic Oath of the fifth century BC:

> I am convinced that if Hippocrates were alive today he would change the wording of his oath... I have a perfectly clear conscience about the part I have played in the affair.

The speaker was Dr Karl Brandt, Hitler's physician, on trial at Nuremberg in 1946.

The debate concerning embryo experiments turned on a number of claims concerning the supposed benefits it would bring in the treatment of infertility and the elimination of handicap, coupled with assertions that the human embryo was not, in any case, a fully fledged member of the human race, and thus not possessed of human rights. If this could be established then, of course, all objections arising from statements of medical ethics like the Helsinki Declaration would disappear. We will therefore examine these claims first.

The start of life

A first impression of this debate concerning the start of life is likely to be one of confusion, with scientists, philosophers and theologians lining up on both sides. The two 'sides', however, are readily distinguished. There are those on the one hand who maintain that fertilisation marks the definitive start of a new human being, and those on the other who say that the question does not really have a precise answer.

Other points such as implantation, 14 days, six weeks, viability, birth and so on are advanced as significant for particular purposes in particular contexts, but no other stage of development commands a significant following as a definite 'now you aren't, now you are' start of existence. Those who for instance, propose 14 days as the significant 'start' are agreed that the 14 days in question are to be measured from fertilisation. None has gone so far as to suggest that the 14th day should be relabelled the first day, and development measured from this point. *The fact that the developmental process begins with fertilisation is really unavoidable.*

One might be forgiven for thinking that the question of the start of life is one of great scientific controversy, or else a question which science cannot usefully illuminate. It is often

The fact that the developmental process begins with fertilisation is really unavoidable.

supposed that the significance of fertilisation is essentially a theological point. The reality is surprisingly different. Even a cursory reading of embryology text books and the scientific literature reveals no doubt at all about the time at which biological life begins. To take a typical example, *The Developing Human*, a text book used widely in medical schools, states:

> Human development is a continuous process that begins when an ovum from a female is fertilised by a sperm from a male . . . a zygote is the beginning of a new human being.[4]

To bring the point home, the first set question in the book is 'When does a new human being begin to develop?' – to which the answer given in the back of the book is 'The development of a human being begins with fertilisation, a process by which a sperm from a male unites with an ovum from a female'.[5]

It would be hard to imagine a simpler or more unequivocal statement of the 'pro-life' position. Numerous further examples from embryology and biology text books can be found. The statement that life begins at fertilisation is a simple statement of scientific fact. There is in reality no controversy and no uncertainty.

The statement that life begins at fertilisation is a simple statement of scientific fact.

The question immediately raised is why, if this is the case, do so many scientists appear on television and in the newspapers denying this fact, and supporting abortion and experimentation on human embryos? Why do they speak of 'grey' areas, 'potential life' and 'pre-embryos?'

The simple answer is that these scientists are applying a double standard. What scientists say in public on this issue and what they write in text books or journals bear little relation to each other. In a purely scientific context the 'start of life' is not a matter of controversy; all is simple and straightforward. It is not until a scientist writes to the newspapers defending his research grant that we hear about 'grey areas' and so forth.

When a scientist says, for example, that a human embryo is 'only a potential life', he really means that he does not think an embryo is very important and he should be allowed to experiment on it. He is making a moral judgement. The danger is that his words are taken as expressing a scientific fact, when in reality the term 'potential life' is biologically meaningless, and appears nowhere in the scientific literature.

Of course scientists are entitled, as we all are, to express a moral view. But in purely moral issues the scientist is no more of an expert than anyone else. By using language in this way, however, the scientist uses his authority as an expert to invest his own moral view (in which he has an undoubted vested interest) with the status of scientific fact. The public will be deceived if it does not understand that he is using language in a very different way from the way he would use it in his professional life.

This double-think within the scientific community is well demonstrated by two articles which appeared in the same issue of the *MRC News* (the magazine of the Medical Research Council) in March 1990. The first, 'Growth control in the developing central nervous system', begins: 'We all started life as a single cell, the fertilised egg, about one tenth of a millimetre in diameter'.[6] This uncontroversial paper concerns pure research into embryology, and refers to experiments on mouse embryos. The term 'embryo' is used throughout: 'pre-embryo' does not appear. The second paper, 'Development of contraceptive vaccine', begins: 'Overpopulation is, arguably, amongst the most important issues currently facing biomedical science'.[7]

The paper refers to the development of a vaccine to prevent human embryos implanting in their mothers' wombs (not, of course a contraceptive, but an abortifacient). The author of this article found it more appropriate to speak of the 'human pre-embryo'.

The use of language in biology today depends crucially upon the politics of the situation.

It must therefore be understood that the use of language in biology today depends crucially upon the politics of the situation. In an uncontroversial context there is no hesitation in referring to the fact known to every biologist: that life begins at fertilisation. No such admissions are made when the aim is to destroy human life. Then we hear the obscurantist language of the 'pre-embryo'.

We shall now discuss briefly some of the more important objections to the idea that life begins at fertilisation.

When life begins is an ethical not a scientific question
This view is stated explicitly in the *Warnock Report*:

> Although the questions of when life or personhood begin appear to be questions of fact susceptible of straightforward answers, we hold that the answers to such questions in fact are complex amalgams of factual and moral judgements.[8]

This argument is probably based upon the observation that a moral question cannot be answered solely in scientific terms. The moral question here is (as Warnock states) 'How it is right to treat the human embryo.' Let us agree that this question cannot be decided on scientific evidence alone. However, the

question of whether the human embryo is an organism and what species it belongs to are definite, scientific questions. If I take an insect to an entomologist, I expect factual answers as to what species it belongs to and whether it is alive or dead, not 'complex amalgams of factual and moral judgements'. The life-status and species-hood of humans is no less definite than that of insects, and this is borne out by the straightforward factual way the question is treated in text books.

Warnock errs (apparently, for nowhere in the *Report* are the deliberations leading to a conclusion given), in assuming that the answer to the question of the humanity of the embryo necessarily decides the moral questions of how to treat it, and must therefore itself have moral content. This is no doubt

The report of the Warnock Committee sparked off a wave of protest against the use of the human embryo for experiments.

because most people would happily argue 'if an embryo is a human being, it is therefore wrong to kill it'. This syllogism is, however, logically incomplete. It requires the almost subconscious moral premise, 'killing human beings is wrong'. The complete argument is:

> (a) An embryo is a human being.
> (b) Killing a human being is wrong.
> therefore: (c) Killing an embryo is wrong.

It is surely clear that proposition (a) is of a purely factual nature, whereas proposition (b) introduces the moral content, allowing a moral conclusion (c) to be reached. It is erroneous to suppose that (a) must have a moral content. Those who accept (a), however, and wish to deny (c) must of course deny (b). It is maybe not surprising that the Warnock Committee wished to gloss over this point.

Life is a continuum, there is no one point at which it begins

This line of argument says that eggs and sperms are alive, that life is a continuum and there is therefore no such thing as the start of life. This relies upon a confusion of terms. The 'start of life' in this context refers to the start of an individual life, not to the creation of life from inanimate matter. It is certainly true that new human beings derive from previously living human beings via living gametes, but this hardly means that individual human beings can have neither a start nor an end. Life is a continuum in the sense that there is a continuous line of living cells linking a man living now with his ancestors who were alive in, say, 1066; but he was not therefore alive in 1066, and is unlikely to be alive in 2066, although his children could be.

Life is a continuum, but individual human beings clearly are not. They have a start and an end. The end is death, and the start is fertilisation.

Fertilisation is not instantaneous

This argument is a favourite of scientists who like to dabble in a little light philosophy. They argue that fertilisation is not an instantaneous event but a process in time, lasting about 20 hours from the penetration of the egg by the sperm to the fusion of the pronuclei at syngamy. On this basis Robert Edwards claims that 'life is continuous' and concludes that '. . . basing any embryological argument, or ethical decision, or legal prohibition upon the moment of fertilisation is dangerously simplistic. No such moment exists'.[9]

Is this true? In the first place one can narrow down the time a

The appeal to life as a continuum – or 'gradualism' – was the main argument employed by the Archbishop of York in debates on the Human Fertilisation and Embryology Bill in the House of Lords. The Archbishop asserted that:

> By and large a biological approach to the beginnings of life is rooted in gradualism ... individual lives ... begin with chemistry and they reach their fulfilment in mystery ... but the transitions on the way to it are not clean, clear and decisive.[10]

However, mystery is not confined to later life nor chemistry to the early stages of life. For many centuries there was no greater mystery than the beginning of life:

John Habgood, Archbishop of York.

> As you do not know the path of the wind,
> or how the body is formed
>   in a mother's womb,
> so you cannot understand
>   the work of God,
>   the Maker of all things.
>
> *Ecclesiastes 11:5*

One of the features of the biblical witness to the incarnate Christ is the mystery which we shall never completely understand, in which the Holy Spirit came upon the Virgin Mary and she conceived the Son of God. This is none other than the mystery revealed to Mary at the Annunciation.

Reference to the Incarnation raises theological arguments to which the Archbishop fails to do justice. He deals only with the difficult and somewhat speculative area of ensoulment. He fails to consider the central theological argument against destructive human embryo research – the Christological argument. Orthodox Christology believes that it was at fertilisation that the Son of God became incarnate. Jesus Christ became man as a human embryo – not later – and if he was at that stage one of us, then so are we all. For he shared complete humanity bar sin. As Nigel Cameron has put it:

> If we accept a classical Christology we will of course want to go much further and affirm that since our Lord took human flesh first as a zygote, so in every zygote there is 'one of us' who bears the *imago Dei*.[11]

The philosophical concept of gradualism finds its theological relation in 'adoptionism' (the belief that Christ became the Son of God gradually, or at a later point in his life, but not at conception). For centuries this has been rejected as heretical. It should remain so.

bit. The significant point is when a sperm penetrates the egg and the zona pelucida (the membrane surrounding the egg) becomes impenetrable to other sperms. It is this irreversible event that determines which of many possible human beings comes into existence.

But this does not address the main point. Whether we narrow down fertilisation to a few hours, a few minutes or a few seconds, it will always be possible to object that we do not have an 'instantaneous' event. The real answer is that it does not matter. There is no event known to physics that is truly instantaneous, but this does not prevent events marking the beginnings or ends of processes.

For example, a speech in Parliament is deemed to begin when an MP stands up to speak. This does not require that his standing up should be instantaneous. There is no instantaneous event that could mark the beginning of a speech, but it would be folly to conclude that the speech never had a start, or will never have an end. A race is said to start when a gun goes off, and the Second World War is often said to have begun with the invasion of Poland. Neither of these events is (or was) instantaneous. The requirement is only that they should be sufficiently short and, more important, that they should have some clear causal connection with what follows. Without these events, the process would not have started at all. In this respect fertilisation marks the start of a new human being admirably, however many hours or minutes it takes.

An embryo is not a human being before 14 days
The Human Fertilisation and Embryology Act (1990) allowed destructive research on human embryos up to 14 days. This time limit arose from the recommendations of the Warnock Committee which reported in 1984. It is most important to understand the reasons for the adoption of this time limit. The reason given in the *Warnock Report* is as follows:

> . . . once the process has begun, there is no particular part of the developmental process that is more important than another; all are part of a continuous process, and unless each stage takes place normally, at the correct time, and in the correct sequence, further development will cease. Thus biologically there is no one single identifiable stage in the development of the embryo beyond which the *in vitro* embryo should not be kept alive. *However we agreed that this was an area in which some precise decision must be taken, in order to allay public anxiety* [emphasis added].[12]

> **The significant point is when a sperm penetrates the egg and the zona pelucida becomes impenetrable to other sperms.**

The *Report* goes on to say that the Royal College of Obstetricians and Gynaecologists had suggested a limit of 17 days, the British Medical Association 14 days, the Medical Research Council and the Royal College of Physicians the end of the implantation stage (about 12 days), and other groups had suggested the start of the implantation stage (about 6 days). The Committee noted that the formation of the primitive streak (a precursor of the neural tube of the embryo) appears at about 15 days and, knocking off a day for good measure, concluded that the limit should be 14 days. The only reason mentioned for considering this point more significant than any other is the novel suggestion that it 'marks the beginning of individual development'.[13] The foundation of this view is discussed in the section on twinning (below). However it is clear that the Warnock Committee did not give much weight to this argument. The choice of a time limit was essentially an arbitrary one which had to be made to 'allay public anxiety'. The arguments that have since been advanced to suggest a definitive importance to the 14 day stage must be seen in this light.

It might be twins!
A supposedly scientific objection to fertilisation as the start of an individual is that in the first few days an embryo may divide entirely in two, or at a slightly later stage may form two babies sharing a placenta. This results in identical twins. The latest stage at which twinning can occur is with the appearance of the primitive streak at about 14 days. As the term 'individual' is said to mean literally 'indivisible', it is contended that the early embryo cannot be an individual. It is often supposed that twinning is a random event, and that therefore until 14 days it is indeterminate how many individuals will result.

While this argument has a superficial plausibility, it is really rather surprising that it should be taken seriously by biologists. Whatever the derivation of the word 'individual', in a biological context it certainly does not mean 'indivisible'. For an organism to divide to produce two separate organisms is one of the commonest processes in nature, and in fact represents the preferred means of reproduction of most simple animals and plants. A good example is the hydra, a small pond-creature well known to GCSE biology students. It is several millimetres in length, and reproduces by budding new hydras from its side. If cut into pieces, each piece will reorganise itself into a new hydra. One never hears of a biologist agonising over whether a hydra is an 'individual', whether it is one, two or several creatures, whether it 'knows' how many hydras it is, or indeed

Whatever the derivation of the word 'individual', in a biological context it certainly does not mean 'indivisible'.

whether it might not be a hydra at all, because it is indeterminate whether it will divide in the next few days. Biologically there is no paradox. A hydra is clearly a single, organised individual creature. If it divides tomorrow, there will then be two hydras. If it does not divide, there will be one, and moreover it will be the same hydra tomorrow as it is today.

Philosophising over the meaning of individuality appears to be the biological equivalent of angels dancing on pins, and such sophistry never appears in serious scientific discussion. Like the non-instantaneousness of fertilisation, the 'continuum of life', the 'grey areas' and the 'pre-embryo', this supposed problem is reserved for the political arena.

Scientifically, there is no reason to hesitate over the idea that a human being can divide just as many other creatures do. This is not behaviour we would expect to observe in an adult, but we all began as single-celled creatures and at that stage behaved as such. Moreover, the process of cloning (successfully carried out on many species of animal, and specifically banned on human beings in the Human Fertilisation and Embryology Act) means that in principle a cell could be taken from any one of us and used to produce an identical clone. This clone would be effectively our identical twin, though of course younger. If the ability to divide means you are not an individual, then none of us is an individual!

If an embryo divides, at that stage it becomes two human beings. If not, it remains the same human being. The argument that the ability to divide means it is not a human being at all is totally without foundation.

A theological variation on this theme questions the time of ensoulment. It is contended that the soul cannot enter the body until the number of people present is determined. We have dealt with the question of ensoulment in Chapter 3 (see pp.39–42), and seen that the soul is the life of the body rather than some kind of separate entity. If one body can become two, we should therefore have no difficulty in accepting that one soul can also become two. But even if it were necessary for an embryo to be endowed with a discrete unalterable number of indivisible souls from fertilisation, the wisdom of God is surely sufficient to provide each embryo with the correct number.

Fourteen days is simply the latest stage at which twinning becomes observable. Although we do not know how identical twinning arises, there is evidence to suggest that it is genetically determined (i.e. established at conception).

Even if it is physically indeterminate whether twinning will occur, the future history of everyone is known to God.

It's only a pre-embryo!
The term 'pre-embryo' is sometimes used to refer to the human embryo up to the appearance of the primitive streak at 14 days. It is used to imply a scientific basis for the notion that up to this stage the embryo is non-human, indeed not even an embryo. For this reason it is most important that the history of the word should be understood.

The term 'pre-embryo' was not used by the embryo experimentation lobby when, in 1984, the *Warnock Report* recommended experimentation upon human embryos up to 14 days. Indeed the term is not found anywhere in the *Warnock Report* itself. It was apparently suggested by a lay member of the Voluntary Licensing Authority (a private body set up by embryo researchers prior to the Human Fertilisation and Embryology Act)[14] and was rapidly taken up by the pro-embryo-research lobby. The definition of this term, which embryologists had previously coped without, exactly coincided with the period of experimentation that the embryo researchers were lobbying for. From the first this raised suspicions that it was a term of convenience, designed to lend retrospective credence to the arbitrary 14-day rule.

It is its reception by the scientific community, however, that is most revealing. In 1987 there was a long correspondence in *Nature*, the world's foremost general science journal. David Davies, a former editor of *Nature* and a member of the Warnock Committee, said that those introducing the term 'pre-embryo' were 'manipulating words to polarise an ethical discussion'.[15] The correspondence culminated in an editorial which, while supporting the recommendations of the Warnock Committee, suggested that the term 'pre-embryo' be banned, adding:

> Put simply, this usage is a cop-out, a way of pretending that the public conflict about IVF and other innovations in human embryology can be made to go away by means of an appropriate nomenclature. The fact is that a fertilised human egg is as deserving of being called an embryo as is a fertilised frog's egg.[16]

'A fertilised human egg is as deserving of being called an embryo as is a fertilised frog's egg.'

This position was endorsed in later letters by a number of scientists. The ban on the term 'pre-embryo' is apparently editorial policy, as papers published on IVF techniques in *Nature* do not use the term.

The majority of early embryos die naturally
It has been repeatedly stated by a number of authorities that, in nature, a very high proportion of fertilised eggs fail to develop

beyond the early stages of pregnancy. The Royal College of Obstetricians and Gynaecologists (RCOG) in a leaflet supporting embryo research, claimed that 'maybe more than two-thirds' of embryos fail to implant. The Medical Research Council (MRC) claimed that 'There is evidence that some 60 per cent of eggs fertilised *in vivo* do not develop beyond the implantation stage'. Lord Walton of Detchant claimed that 'approximately some 80 per cent are spontaneously aborted'.[17]

It has been concluded that this throws doubt upon the proposition that the early embryo is a human being. The reasons for this conclusion are usually obscure. However the Archbishop of York, John Habgood, spelled out one line of reasoning in the House of Lords:

> ... if we face the fact that the majority of fertilised ova never develop beyond a very primitive stage, we seem committed to the curious belief that the majority of souls destined for eternal life will be those whose earthly life has never been anything but embryonic.[18]

It is not clear if the RCOG and MRC were thinking along similar lines.

First, the factual basis of these figures is extremely doubtful. Quoted rates of up to 85 per cent early embryo loss are based upon analyses of data obtained from small numbers of women in the 1940s and 1950s. The most reliable and recent modern study puts early embryo loss, after the stage at which the hormone hCG is produced (6 days), at only 8 per cent. No reliable studies of embryo loss before this stage have been carried out.[19]

The study giving 8 per cent early embryo loss was conducted by the MRC Human Reproduction Group in Newcastle Upon Tyne,[20] which makes it all the more difficult to understand why the MRC and other learned bodies should have been quoting much higher figures during the passage of the Embryo Bill.

Second, it by no means follows that a high rate of natural embryo loss would imply that early embryos were not human beings. Infant mortality has been high throughout most of history, and in many places it still is. The Archbishop of York did not comment on the high proportion of infant souls in heaven. He might as well conclude, on the basis of his own argument, that infants do not have souls. Nor does he explain how he knows that there are not a high proportion of embryonic souls in paradise. Arguments concerning the demography of heaven must surely be considered speculative, unless the Archbishop is claiming to have inside information.

The Archbishop of York might as well conclude that infants do not have souls.

Anger on test tube babies

ARCH ON HUMAN embryos and test tube baby experiments should be ed by a statutory authority — that is the main finding from the Warnock ittee on aritificial reproduction.

ie 16 - member com-
recommendation over
a 14-day limit on
nts on embryos in the
is angered

And the Swansea branch, set
up last summer and con
100 m

Pro-life group hits out at Warnock repor

OVER 200 MPs have
already committed
themselves to fighting
against the use of the
human

protect the human em-
bryo from conception on-
wards against being
used for experimenta-

groups in th
and scientific
activity hav
that it pays d

Chilling thoughts for test-tube theologians

theology has come answers, can be discovered
into fashion, vigorously scratching their
llectual heads. Even the Roman Cath-
lic kind can offer no quick
They tend towards a
ion by means
stiem.

gained that life begins at
conception. Even for those for
whom it is a matter of faith that
life is sacred and should never
be deliberately destro
tific
still

fetuses, babies and adults, of
deep freezing. A conceptus can
be kept, in suitabl

stopped can be started agair
external stimulae.
An organism whose org
processes can be discontir
would not therefore po
"life"; which is another w
saying to lower a
theologian into a vat of l
nitrogen is morally spe
quite different from lowe
two-day old embryo into
so is the resultant inert
an resume its
the

"Guinea pigs" protest

roup has joined a nationwide campaign for legislation to protest
ryos against being used as "guinea pigs."

following the country lobbying M.P.s to
f the con- support a parliamentary
nock Com- campaign for legislation to
the Wilm- protect embryos from con-

munities who wished to
take advantage of the new
supply of human ex-

'Pro-life' MP slams embryo test repor

ly
th
aequ
mpon
)c. Th
digest
they re

NDBURN MP Ken
es, president of
ve Pro-Life
sted

is o
of
so The Govern-
called or
ber

Control these ba experiments — N

vas highly questi
k- genetic tinkering
n worries and fri
) many people in
country."
In the wake o
Warnock Reno
Peacor

Christians respond to Warnock ...

'Halt these test tube experimer

TUBE technology: members of the Warnock
ittee were split over whether experiments
l be performed on live human embryos. The
ian organisations who have responded to thei
are not.
the Methodist Church
of Social Re

AN internationally renowned
geneticist has spoken out against
the use of human embryos for
research.
Prof Jerome Lejeune, from
Paris University, suggested in a
report submitted to the Wo-
mmittee that a
vs of fin
se will
alled

Lejeu
e 19
ch
dro
ese
or
E.

Attack on embryo manipulation

not necessary in the search for a
cure for this or similar diseases.
His statements formed no
a longer report sub
Society

Embryo storm: MP blasts Beeb

i.t
re
un
side
to a
prog
"If
does n
will n
exploita
ement
tor. NAZI-style exper
human embry
rted by the

Must we solve our problems the exper of unbor

MAY I urge read
might be as troubled
Basildo by the Warnock F
ss. write to their MP a
d am deeply disturbe
notion of "spare
nd, insofar as I
arguments pu
ies as muc
as to e
s.

d pul
the essed,
ild areful
p. I recall
ur to the
d myself,
d to at
olutely not
ve been ha
aps I though
was the conse
proposals bef
would never g
Yet once a
into law, cu
wing the oth

Stop these human experiments angry MP

XPERIMENTS where
mster eggs are fer-
ised with human
erm have outraged
stle Point Tory MP
r Bernard Braine.
He says the Warnock com-
ttee report on embryos
d mean lesbians living

was unnecessary to use embryos
in medical research.
Sir Bernard said: "To find a
cure for a genetic disease, it
would be necessary for scientists to produce embryos suffering from it."
"The chance of doing so is
minute, so scientists would first
have to learn how to deform

Ulster urged to fight embryos research

The Ulster public will be
asked today to show pub-
licly its rejection of the
controversial Warnock
Report on research
human emb

a national campaign aimed
at reflecting the stre
of opposition

Legal ban sought on embryo experiments

The start of human life

TH
Bu
Ma

FOLLOWING the issue of
the Warnock Report, King's
Life Group would like

that fertilisation is the starting point of every human life,
hence implantation, quicken-

Therefore those who nerable,
advocate, surrogate beings
motherhood, experimenta- regardl

People do not grieve over embryos as much as over born children

This argument was put forward several times in the House of Lords debate on the Human Fertilisation and Embryology Bill by, among others, Baroness Warnock and the Archbishop of York. The Archbishop said:

> The ordinary response of people dealing with the first fruits of conception — for example, a miscarriage — is sorrow at that event, but one does not say 'There is a human person who has died'. The parents are conscious of their loss. As that conceptus develops into a fetus and eventually into a baby, obviously the consciousness of loss and the value of what has been created increases . . . at different stages we impute different values to what is there in the womb.[21]

Many women who have had miscarriages might dispute some of the Archbishop's assertions. However it is probably true that today most people value unborn life less than born life. The question is how much weight can be attached to this? It has always been the case that people will put widely differing values on the lives of other people, but it would be most unsafe to base the rights of a person in law upon the subjective value accorded to his life by others.

Obviously we will grieve more for a child we have come to know than one we have not known. For this reason we may grieve more over an infant that dies than a fetus. We will certainly grieve more for the death of our own child than the child of someone else, more for the death of a friend or neighbour than for a stranger, and very likely more for a countryman than for a foreign peasant killed in a distant war. Doubtless slave owners grieved more over the death of a white overseer than over the death of a black slave.

Some of these prejudices are inevitable, others are indicative of a deeply unhealthy attitude, but in no case do these personal judgements give us a measure of the real moral worth of the lives concerned. This need not worry us if we are realistic. *Morality does not require us to grieve equally for everyone when they die. It merely requires us not to kill them.*

In a society that condones over 190,000 abortions every year, to rely on these subjective judgements of the value of unborn life to define its status is surely no more than appealing to prejudice to justify prejudice.

An embryo is only a potential human being

As has already been made clear, the fundamental pro-life

argument is that from the moment of fertilisation we are dealing with an actual, living human being. The difficulties of attempting to refute this simple statement of fact have been indicated. This may explain the reluctance of opponents of the pro-life position to face the argument squarely, and their preference for replacing it wherever possible with a nebulous argument of their own devising about 'potential life' and 'potential human beings'. Indeed the *Warnock Report* itself engaged in this sleight-of-hand:

> The human embryo is seen as having the same status as a child or an adult, by virtue of its potential for human life.[22]

The advantages of setting up such a straw man are obvious. Once the claim is weakened to the potential for life, it is hard to distinguish between the potential of the embryo and that of mere eggs and sperms. Moreover, the embryo is given a necessarily inferior status to that of an 'actual' living human being. This device has apparently been very successful, for the notion that the abortion and embryo research debates concern the balance between the rights of 'actual' human beings on the one hand and 'potential' human beings on the other is often stated as if it were a perfectly fair and neutral summary of the opposing positions.

The notion that an embryo is only a potential human being is based upon an elementary confusion. Clearly an embryo has the potential to become a newborn baby, a toddler, and an adult human being. But it by no means follows that it is not a human being in its own right. A toddler has the potential to become an adult, but clearly both are fully and equally human. Each stage of human development has the potential to progress to the later stages, but the term 'human being' applies fully to all of them.

Each stage of human development has the potential to progress to the later stages, but the term 'human being' applies fully to all of them.

The term 'potential human being' could perhaps be applied to eggs and sperm, each of which could potentially fertilise and form a human being. Clearly these 'potential human beings' exist only as possibilities in the minds of those who consider the question, and no one has ever suggested that they have a right to life.

The embryo is not a mere potentiality. It is made of matter: cells, molecules and atoms, that are every bit as real as those that make up the reader, Baroness Warnock or Dr Habgood. After fertilisation we are no longer dealing with a potential human being, but a human being with potential.

The embryo is only a blueprint
This is another argument put forward by the Archbishop of York. He said in an article: 'It would be more accurate to

describe it [the fertilised ovum] as a packet of information, instructions for making a human being, a program which has not been run'. The same point is made by E. O. Wilson: 'The newly fertilised egg . . . is not a human being. It is a set of instructions sent floating into the cavity of the womb'.[23]

In fact the fertilised egg contains one copy of the body's DNA, the same as any other cell. But it is the largest human cell, and the DNA makes up only a tiny fraction of its bulk. It actually contains less DNA, in proportion to its weight, than any other somatic cell, or indeed than an entire adult human being. It would be more accurate to describe Dr Habgood as nothing but a 'packet of information' than the fertilised egg! Certainly the information is important, but the fertilised egg also contains all the machinery for reading that information, carrying out the instructions, and converting itself, stage by stage, into the adult organism. A blueprint is only information, but a blueprint does not grow into a house.

A blueprint is only information, but a blueprint does not grow into a house.

Most of the early embryo is only placenta

This view has been expressed by, among others, Dr Anne McLaren, an animal embryologist, member of the Warnock Committee, Voluntary Licensing Authority, and now the Human Fertilisation and Embryology Authority. She says:

> At the onset of gastrulation, when the human embryo is first formed, it involves less than 1 per cent of the tissue derived from the fertilised egg. The remaining 99 per cent has gone to form the placenta and other nutritive and protective structures.[24]

This observation is again supposed to throw doubt upon the idea that an early embryo is a human being, for reasons that are not adequately explored. The figure of 1 per cent is apparently speculative, but it is true that most of the cells of the early human embryo form the placenta and associated structures. The embryo develops organs as it needs them. The placenta is the first organ of the embryo, and is needed first because it provides the nutrients necessary for further development. The above argument seems to rely upon the assumption that the placenta is not a part of the embryo, and that an embryo that is largely placenta is somehow morally diminished. But as was pointed out by Lord Kennet, even if this assumption were true, 'then 99 per cent of the blob is 100 per cent nothing. And one per cent of it is 100 per cent something'.[25] However it is not at all clear why the placenta should be regarded as any different in principle from the heart or limbs that develop later. The only distinction is that the placenta is required exclusively during the pre-natal period, and is shed at birth. But, during pregnancy, it is as integral a part of the embryo as any other organ, and more important than some other organs, such as the lungs, which are only needed after birth. This argument would appear to be another *non sequitur*.

The triumph of pragmatism

As we have seen, the arguments which seek to deny the humanity of the embryonic human being do not stand up to examination. However the public debate surrounding IVF and embryo research did not hinge on the finer points of philosophy, theology and ethics. The main thrust of the argument, which eventually carried the day with the passage of the Human Fertilisation and Embryology Act (1990), was that the benefits from embryo research would be so great that they had to take precedence over ethical objections. Pro-lifers taking part in television debates would find themselves pitted against mothers with babies conceived by IVF (see box). Newspaper coverage featured handicapped people who were under the impression that their suffering could have been prevented by embryo research.[26] The pro-life position was thus made to appear heartless.

However, it is important to remember that there is no other area in which the argument would be accepted that the interests of society should take precedence over the interests of the person on whom the research is being carried out.

For example, the only way to obtain reliable data about the reaction of human beings to cold water is to immerse human beings and measure their vital signs. Some data may be obtained with the help of volunteers, but the criteria of severe hypothermia can only be investigated at great risk to the subject. This was indeed done by Nazi doctors with subjects obtained from concentration camps, many of whom died.[27] While much of this data is worthless, some is used even today in the design of marine survival equipment. No other source of data is available. Even this use of the data to save lives is controversial, given the now universal view that such experiments were an atrocious crime against humanity. Clearly it would be irrelevant, if such experiments were being proposed today, to consider whether more people would be saved by the survival equipment than would die in the experiments.

In most cases research can proceed by ethical means. If it cannot, that is just too bad.

In most cases research can proceed by ethical means. If it cannot, that is just too bad. It is not an excuse for rewriting the rule book.

In the Warnock Report the argument for *in vitro* fertilisation was almost entirely based on the plight of infertile couples.[28] No one would deny the heartache and misery of infertility, although we need to be aware that abortion is a major cause both of infertility and of the scarcity of babies for adoption.

However, even those embryos created with a view to transferring them to the womb (as opposed to those created specifically for experiments) have only a very slim chance of developing to birth and beyond. Of those actually transferred to the womb only 7 out of every 100 will survive to be born.[29]

Respect and care are due to our progeny from the beginning of their development and IVF runs against this. It is open to the following serious objections:

- IVF babies risk being denied transfer to the womb: they are either discarded, frozen or used for research;

- The long-term consequences for babies' health, life-span, psychological welfare, etc, cannot be predicted: the present generation of IVF children are guinea-pigs who must be monitored throughout their lives;

- The complex processes before, during and immediately after fertilisation are managed by nature in a uniquely receptive environment — the mother's reproductive system — providing physical protection, temperature control, appropriate chemical conditions and shielding from light/radiation. IVF practitioners try to make appropriate substitutions for the mother's body,[30] but the relative importance of these critical factors is not fully understood;

- IVF replaces women as the sole custodians of human conception and gestation in the role of motherhood, which is their inheritance and privilege. (Many feminists reject IVF as a technological intrusion into women's bodies).[31]

The point here is that IVF is wrong, and not simply because it may or will lead to abuses of embryonic life, most of which would be impossible without IVF. Rather, we say that to make someone — in this case an embryo — vulnerable to such practices is degrading and wrong in itself.

There is an understandable but mistaken idea that couples have a 'right' to have a child. Such a 'right' implies that the child exists to fulfil the desires of the parents. Many children do, of course, fulfil their parents' longing, but they have a right to be and a purpose in being that goes beyond that. The suggestion that the couple's desire must always be fulfilled cannot be squared with the scriptural understanding of life — especially the life of a child — as a gift from God.

Research v. ethics

One of the most alarming aspects of the embryo research debate has been the apparent failure of both Houses of Parliament to understand the relationship between medical research and medical ethics. Statements that restrictions on research would hold back 'progress' were widely regarded as conclusive, as if no further justification were needed for embryo research. But *all* ethical guidelines hold back research. Doubtless every area of medical research could benefit from destructive experiments on human subjects.

In cancer research, for example, it might be highly effective to test treatments upon properly controlled groups with deliberately induced cancers. Subjects could be killed and autopsied to investigate the progress of the disease, and control groups could be denied treatment for comparison. This is exactly what is done with animals.

The reason that this is not done with humans is not because it would be poor science, but simply because it would be wrong. Of course most medical researchers do not consciously regard the Declaration of Helsinki as a hindrance. No one would even consider destructive experiments upon human beings in the normal course of research. But uniquely, in the case of embryo research, the possibility has been considered and accepted by Parliament when it passed the Human Fertilisation and Embryology Act (1990). Research on human embryos was declared legal, whether the embryos were 'spare embryos' left over from IVF procedures, or embryos created specifically to be experimented on. They can be used to test drugs and to develop new contraceptives.

However, the promises which were made during the progress of the Act have so far proved empty. IVF remains an expensive and ineffective procedure, and the wild threats of genetic screening of embryos have so far come to nothing (for which we may be thankful). The passage of the Act, however, represents a break with traditional medical ethics, of which the repercussions will become more important as time goes on. It appears that by obscuring the issues and appealing to 'progress', the scientific community can now extract from Parliament a licence to do whatever it chooses.

Every area of medical research could benefit from destructive experiments on human subjects.

CHAPTER EIGHT

Handicapped children

Let us make man in our image, in our likeness.
Genesis 1:26

In 1990 British abortion legislation was changed by the Human Fertilisation and Embryology Act. A time limit was introduced into abortion law for the first time (see Chapter 5), fixing an upper limit of 24 weeks of pregnancy. However there were to be exceptions to this limit to allow abortion up to birth for those falling within certain categories. Handicapped babies were specifically included within these exceptional categories. For many people, including Members of Parliament and even active members of the Christian churches, the horror of bearing a handicapped child was great enough to outweigh the natural revulsion which people feel towards very late abortions, which involve the deliberate destruction and sometimes the gruesome physical dismemberment of a completely formed child who would, in many cases, be able to survive outside the womb if permitted to live.

This must be seen alongside the fact that over the last 25 years developing medical technology has significantly increased the amount of knowledge about the unborn child to which a doctor has access during pregnancy, including the possible presence of disability. **More and more pregnancies are falling into the category of cases for which termination is permissible at any stage.** Within the Church, the same exception has been cited: as early as 1967 the then Archbishop of Canterbury, Michael Ramsey, listed the case of a handicapped fetus among his stated exceptions to the inviolability of the unborn child.

The gravity of the present situation was pointed out by the Archbishop of York when he observed that now 'seriously handicapped people may be destroyed simply because they are seriously handicapped'.[1] This demands a response from evangelicals, a response which is based on biblical principles, which begins to explore a theology of disability and handicap and which offers the foundations of an ethical critique of those views now prevalent which state that evidence of handicap is sufficient reason to terminate life in the womb.

The pitfalls of screening

There are thorny issues around the use of ante-natal diagnostic techniques; problems and considerations which need to be taken seriously. At its best, ante-natal diagnosis can provide parents and families with the opportunity to prepare for the birth of a baby who will have particular difficulties and corresponding needs. It can also allow medical teams to give the mother and child the best support possible during pregnancy and birth. (Increasingly one such option is intra-uterine surgery, which is currently developing.)

More frequently, however, the assumption – or even requirement – is that a woman who undergoes these tests will agree to an abortion should they prove positive. As the techniques become more commonplace in ante-natal care, women increasingly have to assert themselves should they wish not to go through with pre-natal testing. In other words, the default option is shifting, putting the onus on women to refuse tests rather than their having to qualify for them. A problematic power dynamic is set up, then, with which many women are not equipped to deal. Of course there are exceptions and some medical personnel take time and trouble to explain the options comprehensibly and fully, but this is not the general trend.

Some ante-natal diagnostic techniques themselves carry inherent dangers such as increasing the likelihood of miscarriage, although there is no agreement as to the statistical details. Also, there are problems regarding the accuracy of the techniques, with their tendency to give both false positive and false negative results, either of which can cause a good deal of unnecessary suffering for the mother and child.

There are problems regarding the accuracy of the techniques, with their tendency to give both false positive and false negative results.

Clearly, these issues are important, carrying implications for Christians and demanding a practical response. For instance, how many mothers who are told that their unborn child has Down's Syndrome know a family which includes a person with Down's Syndrome? If they did, might it not affect their attitude towards their child? A network of families who can talk to pregnant women could go a long way towards alleviating ignorance and misunderstanding. Similarly, the offer of counselling or even just information presented in an accessible way could help to inform mothers of the implications of their test results and of the prognosis for their child.

However, even assuming tests which are 100 per cent accurate, and decision-making which is genuinely informed and autonomous, there are major philosophical and theological problems with the process of ante-natal screening and ensuing 'therapeutic' abortion.

Disabled or handicapped

In *Disability: Whose Handicap?* Ann Shearer gives a useful analysis of the semantics of disability and handicap. She talks of 'handicap' when it is confronted by a society which imposes limits upon it. She asks whether 'the inability to run to catch a bus [or] go up and down stairs . . . [would] still make a person "handicapped" if the buses waited for their passengers [and] ramps replaced the stairs?'.[2] This provides us with an underlying premise of any acceptable theology of handicap since it clearly lays the responsibility at the feet of society and not with the disabled person. As Christians we must take seriously the fact that, in principle, many of the problems and difficulties which people with disabilities have are not insurmountable. And this is not only true of practical difficulties; it is also true of emotional and psychological problems. Research clearly shows, and a large body of literature backs up the theory, that depression, embarrassment and discomfort as experienced by people with disabilities and by their families and friends are largely due to the attitude of other people: such trauma is not inherently down to the disability itself, whatever it might be.[3]

The tyranny of the 'normal'

What we are dealing with here, then, are stigmas and the idea of being 'normal'. What counts as normal? And how do we treat those who fall outside our definition of the normal? Note the arbitrary and relative nature of the definitions: until recently left-handedness was regarded as a disability, and conversely only with improvements in educational provisions has illiteracy come to be seen as a handicap. Christians have a vital contribution to make to the debate about what is 'normal'.

There is a sense in which we are all 'disabled'.

There is a sense in which we are all 'disabled'. We all need to be aware of our own limitations and adjust our expectations accordingly. In this sense, disability is relative to a perceived ideal state compared with which we are all lacking. Theologically, this resonates with the doctrine of the Fall, since we are none of us as God intended us to be; we are living in the not-yet-of-God's kingdom and awaiting restoration to complete wholeness. We are constantly faced with evidence for, and the results of, this fact not least in our physical nature. The whole of

creation is 'groaning as in the pains of childbirth' and we, too 'groan inwardly as we wait eagerly for our adoption as sons, the redemption of our bodies' (Rom. 8:22–23).

Such a view of universal disability is problematic because it runs counter to the way in which the term is generally used. In common usage the word 'disabled' is taken to stand opposed to the term 'able-bodied'. Each of us fits into one category or the other and there is generally little doubt as to which it is. A network of ante-natal tests which gives a diagnosis *in utero* encourages us to categorise the unborn child in the same way. It can be labelled 'handicapped', 'deformed' or 'defective' and little thought is given to the prognosis for the specific case.

Quality control
Alongside this labelling and categorising, the concept of *quality of life* is at work. There is an assumption in much secular thought, and increasingly in Christian ethical systems, that it is possible for someone's *quality of life* to degenerate to such a low level that life is not worth living.

Handicapped members of SPUC and their families organised a picket of the Medical Research Council as a protest against drug trials which failed to respect their rights.

At the other end of the spectrum, we generally want to improve our own quality of life as much as possible, as well as that of the people we care about. Maybe we are altruistic enough to want to improve the quality of life of other people too, even if it involves some personal cost. Parents, in the great majority of cases, want the best possible quality of life for their children. This is straightforward and unproblematic. Until, that is, parents are urged to think of quality of life as a distinct commodity which must be maximised in their child; if this particular unborn child cannot attain a minimum quality of life then it is acceptable to terminate the pregnancy in order to achieve a better quality of life in a future pregnancy.

Quality of life has become more important than the person by whom it is experienced.

The commodity, quality of life, has become more important than the person in whom it is expressed and by whom it is experienced. This, along with the closely linked argument that abortion can be 'for the sake of the unborn child', is logically very odd.

A situation has been created in which parents regard the birth of a 'normal' baby as a right. This is especially worrying when seen in the light of the argument that quality of life, for someone with a disability, may be more about society than it is about the individual.

It is the concept of 'normal' which underpins our attitude to those we call 'disabled' and to those unborn children labelled as 'handicapped' or 'defective'. Normality is being defined in ever more restrictive ways, and is gradually coming closer to that theoretical ideal against which we define pathology. This ideal has traditionally been regarded as unattainable, but with the ability to see *in utero* we can screen out those babies who most spectacularly fall short of the ideal. What we regard as normal, and therefore tolerable, is changing as the technology develops to change existing people and prevent the birth of suspect babies.

Babies or artefacts?

Oliver O'Donovan in *Begotten or Made?*[4] characterises a technological society not by what it does or even can do but by its attitudes. He regards our society as technological because it sees everything as an artefact: machinery and scientific knowledge certainly, but also history, for instance – and children. Artefacts can be altered, acted upon, dispensed with. If a child is an artefact it can be (indeed should be) improved, enhanced and dismissed if it cannot reach a certain standard. Those people who most obviously fall short of the ideal (from which we all deviate) are labelled 'abnormal'; they are in need of our support in the form of charity and other special provision; they are different from the rest of us. Only a certain amount of deviation from the norm is tolerated, indeed an increasingly small amount of deviation is tolerated, before a cut-off point is reached. Beyond that point an individual child is regarded as having forfeited its inviolability and right to legal protection. The process of eliminating the bottom of the pile is, by definition, endless since there will always be someone, or a group of people, in that position.

Narrowing the gate

This narrowing of the concept of what is 'normal' is insidiously self-perpetuating. 'Unsightly' birth marks can be treated with laser technology; surgery can alter the characteristic facial appearance which is associated with Down's Syndrome; major orthopaedic surgery can be offered to correct scoliosis and kyphosis (curvature of the spine) often with an emphasis on the cosmetic benefits. In exactly the same way, improved ante-natal diagnosis allows doctors to offer parents the option of destroying unborn children with a disabling condition.

All of these techniques serve to squeeze the concept of 'normal' more tightly still. How much greater is the stigma carried by a woman unable, for whatever reason, to undergo laser treatment for a birth-mark or by a child born with spina bifida in a society which believes itself able to deal with these 'problems'? And what incentive is there to improve intra-uterine surgery when a much more straightforward option is to abort?

As the concept of the normal grows ever tighter, so does our understanding of what it is for a person to flourish and we start to confuse needs and desires. A body 'needs' not only to function adequately (which in itself is relative to society's physical structures) but it 'needs' to function well and to look acceptable, even beautiful.

So what is to be our response to the detection of a condition such as spina bifida in an unborn child? It must lie along two complementary but distinct paths: first an analysis of the prognosis for the child and an investigation of what a Christian approach can do by way of alleviating problems; and second a look at what God communicates to us about his attitude to such unborn children.

The prognosis obviously depends to some extent on a medically informed judgement. However, the prognosis for social integration and progress depends on other factors. Let us assume that the unborn child has spina bifida and has certain

The SPUC Educational Research Trust raises funds for research into Down's Syndrome through the Anna Fund. The Fund is named in memory of Anna McKean, seen here with her grandmother Margaret White, Vice President of SPUC.

This narrowing of the concept of what is 'normal' is insidiously self-perpetuating.

inherent problems because of the medical facts – perhaps paralysis from the waist down and associated incontinence, a vulnerability to infection and possibly hydrocephalus with intellectual impairment.

The reproach of the imperfect

Medically, this child will always be something of a 'rogue' since she will be a constant reminder of the fallibility and ultimate impotence of even the most sophisticated technology and medical science. Significant sections of the medical community will insisit that she be eliminated before (or soon after) birth in order that we, as a society, can claim success in 'conquering' spina bifida – a laudable goal, after all. Financially, too, the child will be a rogue, since studies suggest that the cost of supporting her and others like her will exceed the cost of the screening programme which has sought her out.

This perspective is uncomfortably close to a view which is prepared to sacrifice the individual for the sake of the society of which she is part. However, as Bernard Palmer stresses in *Medicine and the Bible*, as Christians we have a mandate to 'curtail disease to save life but not to curtail life to restrict disease'.[5] Otherwise we find ourselves falling foul of that most basic ethical principle which tells us to treat humanity, whether in our own person or in that of another, always as an end and never as a means only.

There is a temptation to label the disabled baby as 'Other', in order to defuse the threat which she now poses and will increasingly pose as her life continues. An imperfect body will be a stark reminder of the fragility of physical health and of life itself. Seeing a child's paralysed body offensively reminds us of our own morbidity and mortality, so we find it easier to give her the label 'deformed', thereby putting a distance between us. Even supposing that she manages to achieve a level of joy and fulfilment in her 'damaged' life, that will be unpalatable because our fundamental value system will then be threatened: how can someone fall so far short of our ideal and yct still have an existence which is positive? Is our ideal all it is cracked up to be? Our defensive response is to isolate this child and regard her as a courageous heroine; we will, in other words, affirm the rule by drawing attention to the exception.

Christians are not immune to the psychological threats posed by people with disabilities but do we need to succumb to them? Surely we can face our own fallibility and impotence, our own mortality and morbidity, knowing that Christ has robbed death of its power over us. This frees us to relate to those whom

As Christians we have a mandate to 'curtail disease to save life but not to curtail life to restrict disease'.

society finds embarrassing or offensive, and to discover within them the unique image of God which they carry.

Neither do we need to follow the trend of dividing people into the 'weak' and 'the capable'. The body of Christ is about giving and receiving in dynamic relationships, not assigning static, immutable roles. A Christian society is composed of people who are prepared to acknowledge their vulnerability and weakness just as God himself has done in the Incarnation.

Prayers for healing

If handicapped children do continue to grow and develop, they may well come across Christians who have a theology of sickness which urges them to pray for them: these children do not need to be as they are and God wants to heal them. Christian theology is a theology of the flesh in that the eternal word 'became flesh and dwelt among us'. God cares about our bodies and weeps with us in our physical suffering; he can and does give healing in this life, but we need to be clear about the status of sickness in the kingdom of God.

The Bible does not talk of heaven as a place without any sick people, but as a place without sickness itself (Rev. 21:3–4; Isa. 35:5–6). The sick will be restored, the blind will see; we are not to eradicate the sick and the blind and fool ourselves into thinking that we are thereby brought closer to God's kingdom. We need to be very careful too about our motives as we pray for people to be healed. Who has the bigger problem – the person with a disability or the Christian, eager to pray for healing, who somehow has a view of God's kingdom on earth blemished by the presence of imperfect bodies and minds? And what are we saying to people who use wheelchairs when we shout triumphally about casting them aside?

There is a real danger that as we insist on praying for the healing of people with disabilities we overlook the respect and love which are due to them as part of God's creation. This is essentially the same difficulty that is faced by anyone, Christian or not, who supports the abortion of handicapped babies and yet purports to respect and value disabled members of society.

Made in God's image

Perhaps the most fundamental question we need to ask is whether there is any circumstance which can rob an individual of the image of God. Can any medical condition make that person unworthy of an intimate relationship with him and with the rest of humanity? There are those who ask 'why an anencephalic infant more closely resembles God than, say, a

Perhaps the most fundamental question we need to ask is whether there is any circumstance which can rob an individual of the image of God.

Perhaps one of the most disturbing aspects of current abortion practice in Britain confronting Christians is the fact that the abortion of disabled babies is being increasingly proposed and promoted by Government bodies, independent bodies and some sections of the medical profession as a cost-saving measure.

For example, in 1976 the Department of Health published a book to mark the launch of a major screening programme of amniocentesis and abortion of disabled babies which included the following justification for the programme:

> Apart from the medical conditions to which they are prone in infancy and childhood, mongol children may require, as many do, eventually to be cared for in institutions imposing a further heavy burden on the health service ... The grossly handicapped spina bifida child and adult makes large demands on the health and social services. It seems likely that, in general, the cost of these demands will exceed the cost of a programme to detect the condition.[7]

Thus the handicapped child and adult were seen merely as debits on the state ledger — not as individuals with needs and rights.

In the same vein, the doctors working at St Bartholomew's Hospital in London in 1992 announced a new blood test for pregnant women which could detect Down's Syndrome in the womb and which, they boasted, would save the country £82,000 in upkeep for every affected baby killed before birth.[8]

A chilling report from the Office of Health Economics in 1993 observed that:

> Genetic disorders place considerable health and economic burdens not only on affected people and their families but also on the community as a whole.[9]

The report described 'genetic counselling' for couples planning to reproduce, on the grounds that many genetic and hereditary disorders can be predicted in advance. Advances in 'gene mapping' may lead to extremely accurate forecasts of the life expectancy of individuals, even before they are born. One suggestion put forward for discussion was that a woman who knowingly gave birth to a disabled child could be 'held accountable' and made to pay the health costs herself.[10]

> In the same way one is required to take a test before being allowed to drive a car, a test may be required before one is deemed suitably able to give birth.[11]

This approach to handicap as a matter of financial gain or loss for society is not new. In Nazi Germany it was a major consideration behind the euthanasia programme, which included amputees from the First World War among its handicapped victims. Adolf Hitler wrote in *Mein Kampf*:

> It [the People's State] must see to it that only those who are healthy shall beget children ... In this matter that State must assert itself as the trustee of a millennial future ... Those who are physically and mentally unhealthy and unfit must not perpetuate their own suffering in the bodies of their children.[12]

As Christians, we have a special duty to consider the historical parallels of allowing life to be assessed in purely financial terms and to recognise how the same philosophy leads, inexorably, to euthanasia. Parents, as well as unborn babies, increasingly become victims of this sort of philosophy as the economic pressures on the health service increase and as tests for handicap become more and more widely available.

pig'[6] – a startling comparison. Are we prepared to go along with this, or is it rather the case that the child – born or unborn – with a severe disability is still made by God (Exod. 4:11–12) and can say, together with able-bodied peers, 'you knit me together in my mother's womb. I praise you because I am fearfully and wonderfully made; your works are wonderful, I know that full well' (Ps. 139:13–14)?

This is clearly the single most important point of principle which a Christian can contribute to the argument concerning the handicapped unborn. But it is not the only contribution: speaking out against the abortion of the handicapped unborn necessarily implicates us in changing an intolerant society and in supporting families who are facing what they are encouraged to believe is a tragedy.

The widow, the orphan – and the unborn

Biblical standards are shocking and radical, teaching us that it is those who are most vulnerable who are especially deserving of our respect and protection (Lev. 19:14; Deut. 27:18; Ps. 82:3–4):

Biblical standards are shocking and radical.

> Speak up for those who cannot speak for themselves,
> for the rights of all who are destitute.
> Speak up and judge fairly;
> defend the rights of the poor and needy.
>
> *Proverbs 31:8-9*

The teaching of Jesus encourages us to approach our fellow human beings in relationship. It is in this light that we must judge the calls to abort the handicapped unborn child.

This whole issue has massive implications for, and is massively affected by, our fundamental beliefs about God and humanity. It demands a considered response, not only through statements of belief about the ethics of aborting the handicapped unborn, but also through out entire lives as they testify to our God of vulnerability and redemption, the God of our created, physical world who counts our tears and stores them in a bottle as he weeps with us in our fallen, but never unreachable, human condition.

CHAPTER NINE

Abortion's other victims

A voice is heard in Ramah,
mourning and great weeping,
Rachel weeping for her children
and refusing to be comforted,
because her children are no more.
Jeremiah 31:15

The evidence that abortion can affect the mental health of women has been accumulating for some time. The 1975 Danish study (see p.87) indicated that women who had undergone abortions were significantly more likely to be admitted to psychiatric hospitals than those who had not, and a review article in the *British Journal of Psychiatry* found that approximately 10 per cent of women having an abortion will suffer marked, severe or persistent psychological or psychiatric disturbances.[1]

The 1980s witnessed an increasing interest among mental health professionals in the possibility of identifying symptoms of post-traumatic stress disorder which could be linked to abortion. The phenomenon of Post Abortion Syndrome (PAS) has been increasingly discussed in professional journals and studies[2] and within professional organisations. A number of books have also examined the accumulating evidence.[3]

However, despite the enormous number of letters published in newspapers and women's magazines from women recounting their own trauma and suffering following abortion, the subject of Post Abortion Syndrome remains controversial. Some mental health experts and their professional associations even deny that it exists. This is partly because most of the major health organisations of the western world have allied themselves firmly to the pro-abortion cause. They are therefore professionally committed to minimising the possible ill-effects of the procedure, which must at the very least be kept to a level at which they would seem to be 'worth the risk', given the stated 'advantages' of abortion.

Most of the major health organisations of the western world have allied themselves firmly to the pro-abortion cause.

Abortion activists and their allies in the media have been unwilling to give credence to the growing volume of evidence that women have suffered serious consequences to their mental health as a result of abortion. This is because, as the authors of a study in the *Journal of Social Work and Human Sexuality* pointed out in 1985, they fear that any admission of the negative consequences of abortion will provide ammunition to pro-life campaigners.[4]

To complicate matters further there is a lack of consensus among professionals regarding the symptoms, severity and duration of mental disorder which could be used to characterise PAS, as well as a seriously flawed methodology in many of the studies. For example, no major scientific body has carried out any research which follows women for more than one year after their abortion, and yet the symptoms of PAS often do not manifest themselves for *five to ten years or more* after the abortion.

This unwillingness to examine the problems which it is at least reasonable to assume would flow from a violent intervention in the process of human reproduction is extraordinary, given the increasing awareness of the sensitivity of all ecological mechanisms. As Canadian psychiatrist Philip Ney puts it:

While the experts differ, the women suffer.

When we are so careful not to tamper with the delicate balance of plant and animal ecology, one wonders why we do not at least study the far-reaching effects that killing unborn infants may be having on the human species.[5]

While the experts differ, the women suffer. The scale of the problem is difficult to appreciate. With nearly four million abortions carried out in Britain between 1967 and the end of 1992, and over one and a half million *every year* in the USA, the global figure is put at anything between thirty and fifty million abortions a year. It is one of the most frequently performed surgical procedures in the world. Consequently, any ill-effects will manifest themselves on a huge scale.

Throughout the 1980s women were coming together, trying to find help and to help each other in coping with the feelings of pain, anger, fear, hurt and loss which go with abortion. Many of these women had experienced disruption in their relationships, uncontrolled re-experiencing of the abortion event, and feelings of guilt and depression verging on the suicidal. In this way, through the informal networking of injured women, associations were formed throughout America, the UK and other countries to alleviate the distress and to warn others of the real nature of abortion.

British Victims of Abortion (BVA) was one of these associations. Formed in 1987, it has worked to bring women to a position of healing. Also, it needs to be remembered that women are not the only 'other' victims of abortion: their husbands, partners, parents and surviving children can all suffer as a result of the abortion experience. In a sense every one of us is affected and diminished because other members of the human race are killed by abortion and our society is brutalised. The need for healing is great.

The following account has been compiled by a member of BVA and draws directly on the personal experiences of other members. For obvious reasons they have requested that their anonymity in such intimate matters be respected.

*　　*　　*

The need for healing

No one would dispute that one of the main tenets of the Gospel is that through acknowledging our wrong doings we may receive absolution and forgiveness. We hear frequent sermons exhorting us to repent and receive forgiveness with the promise that we can walk in newness of life. I neither doubt nor question the validity of this Gospel message but I do wonder for how many this is a personal reality. For many, the Church has failed to help because of its failure to speak out on the issue of abortion.

For many, the Church has failed to help because of its failure to speak out on the issue of abortion.

During the last few years of involvement with BVA I and others involved in the counselling and supporting of women who have had abortions have seen much trauma and suffering. Many women have carried their pain for years, keeping it secret and allowing that hidden wound to fester.

In this chapter I hope to look at several key issues for women as they struggle towards healing from their abortion experience. In looking at this struggle it is also crucial to begin to examine the role of the Church and to see the ways in which we as Christians can enable, encourage and love the often forgotten victims of abortion – the women.

The context

The crisis pregnancy

Our experience over the years in BVA has shown us that calm rational thought has little place in the minds of women who confront crisis pregnancies.

All I could think of was I have a problem, I must get rid of it.

My mind constantly tried to deny this pregnancy. I used all kinds of excuses – I had a tummy bug, I had misread the test, anything at all to deny the reality of the life within me.

I myself have often heard women who have chosen to resolve their pregnancy by having an abortion described as uncaring, selfish, and unthinking. Our experience of counselling women in BVA has shown them to be largely women who are in a desperate situation and who adopt a desperate solution. Because of the crisis few women want to hear the reality of what they are about to do and, by the nature of the 'counselling' they receive, even fewer get that information.

In the course of our work in BVA we frequently hear of minimal information being given by the many clinics and agencies that claim to provide informed counselling.

*'My counselling lasted
less than ten minutes.'*

I wasn't counselled, I was simply told it would be best for me and my future to have an abortion.

My counselling lasted less than ten minutes.

Few women are confronted with the perhaps harsh reality that they are carrying a living human being. Instead they are fobbed off with vague terms and platitudes which perpetuate the denial of life.

So in the midst of the crisis, with often inadequate counselling, little emotional support and with the pregnancy often a secret, the woman sees abortion as the solution – the simple way out, or so she hopes!

I went into the anaesthetic having arrived at a kind of truce with myself – that life would be OK and would go on as normal. I woke up screaming with pain with the realisation that life could never be the same again.

Keeping the secret

If you are unable to face the pain, you are faced with little alternative but to deny the trauma in order to survive. There are often no resources to begin looking at the issues involved and there is the implicit taboo: 'I have committed a terrible crime, I must keep it secret'. The secret is maintained by the woman herself, by society – 'let's not talk about this, it isn't a problem' – and by the Church which, through its silence, aids and abets such thinking.

As Christians, we have the responsibility to make heard the

injustice and wrongs of abortion, but we must say these things in a manner which is clear yet compassionate. If we do, it will enable women to begin to speak of their experiences in the knowledge that the way is open for their healing to begin.

American singing star Pat Boone joined MPs and SPUC members to form a pro-life chain around London on 24 April 1993. The chain included members of British Victims of Abortion.

Post Abortion Syndrome (PAS)

In recent years both research and counselling have led to the identification of symptoms that can be described as Post Abortion Syndrome (PAS). Many women experience several of the following symptoms after an abortion:

- re-experiencing the abortion in recurrent dreams/memories
- a sense of detachment from others
- a reduced ability to express feelings
- depression
- overwhelming guilt
- sleep disturbance
- memory impairment
- eating disorders

- sexual dysfunction

- low self-esteem

The catalogue of consequences can go on and on and it is often with a sense of relief that women come to BVA and discover that their symptoms can be related to the abortion experience.

> I didn't know whether to be relieved or saddened when I confronted the criteria for PAS because I was reading about me!

The beginning of healing

> You will surely forget your trouble,
> recalling it only as waters gone by.
> Life will be brighter than noonday,
> and darkness will become like morning.
> You will be secure, because there is hope;
> you will look about you and take your rest in safety.
>
> *Job 11:16–18*

PAS encompasses the mourning, guilt, pain and grief that have been denied. The longer a woman denies her abortion and her responsibility for it, the more intense her reactions to the abortion. The basis of her denial is the fact that abortion took the life of her child and she allowed it to happen. Confronting the death of a child is the first step to healing. Denying the death denies the sinful act, causing a separation from God.

Confronting the death of a child is the first step to healing.

Denial can take many forms. The woman who has no conscious awareness of the pain or loss may even say, 'I never had an abortion'.

> Even when I was pregnant with my first child from my marriage, I answered 'no' to the question 'Have you had a termination?', and I believed my answer.

Some women block the abortion trauma whenever they find themselves in a situation where they are reminded of the abortion. They do not grieve because whenever feelings surface they are denied.

Denial can also manifest itself with distractions, using activities as an outlet for anxiety, in effect making life so busy that there is no time for dealing with the trauma.

Women often have their denial reinforced by those around them. It is a common misconception that it makes a woman feel better to reassure her that:

- it wasn't that 'bad' a thing to do;

- it's all over and forgotten;

- time heals everything.

Time and time again I have heard women's distress at being 'prevented' from moving out of denial. What needs to be heard is:

- the abortion was wrong and that as a result a child has lost the gift of life;

- it can be over, the nightmare can end, but it will not be (neither should it be!) forgotten;

- time alone does not heal everything, only by engaging in the healing process can there be resolution.

> My healing began the day I acknowledged the death of my child and no longer referred to her as a fetus. I made her a person, I gave her a name.

Acknowledging the child is important, and as time moves on it can actually be a comfort to know that there was a person who was once real and alive.

Guilt and anger

For many, the overriding feeling that drives them into seeking help is one of guilt. That feeling can range from a barely acknowledged sense of wrong to a crippling, all-consuming emotion that encompasses a woman's life.

It would be easy at this point to produce scriptures about forgiveness a bit like a magician producing a rabbit from a hat, but first the point of 'letting go' has to be reached. Maintaining guilt can seem a legitimate way to keep punishing yourself. It is easier perhaps to allow yourself to remain bound by feelings of guilt than to face the fact that you can be forgiven. Women do not need the finger of harsh judgement to be pointed at them; they are often their own harshest and most condemning judges.

Guilt and anger at times can walk hand in hand. Anger is an emotion that few of us are truly comfortable with and it often bubbles away beneath the surface. Anger in the context of the abortion experience is something that will be awakened in counselling, but it is a little like waking a sleeping monster! Although much of the anger is legitimate it must be constructively harnessed.

Women do not need the finger of harsh judgement to be pointed at them; they are often their own harshest and most condemning judges.

Anger usually occurs when a woman realises that much of what she was told was lies:

> My anger surfaced when I realised it was not a 'mass of tissue' but a tiny human being complete with fingers and toes and a heart that really works.

> I hit the roof when I saw the fetal models. Why had no one told me or shown me at the clinic?

> The more I found out about the string of physical effects the greater my rage at the doctors who kept me in ignorance.

To be confronted with the fact that there were alternatives when it is too late is hard to face.

Anger is also directed at the people involved in the decision-making process: parents, the baby's father, a friend, counsellors at the clinic. To be confronted with the fact that there were alternatives when it is too late is hard to face.

Anger does not just confine itself to the obvious target – the doctors, clinics, hospitals and counsellors. Anger can be directed at the world for the injustice of abortion. There can be anger at God for allowing the pregnancy and the abortion to occur, and anger at the unborn child for being conceived. Subsequent children may suffer for having survived when the aborted child did not.

At the bottom of what at times can appear to be a mountain of anger is the anger a woman feels towards herself. She is angry because she has allowed her unborn child to be killed and she didn't save it. She is angry at saying yes to an abortion. She is often angry because she is alive and her child isn't. Counsellors walk a tightrope between helping a woman acknowledge and express appropriate anger and not allowing this to fuel further pain and self-punishment.

Grieving

We have looked a little at the need to acknowledge the child. It is also a major part of the healing process to grieve and mourn the loss of that child. Dysfunction occurs when that grief is not allowed. Because abortion is so often a secret, it is hard to follow the natural process of mourning.

> It was twenty years after my abortion that I began to cry for my child and to mourn the loss.

> It was like opening the floodgates: I felt engulfed by a raw torrent of pain. This was my long-held grief. I was glad to feel the pain, it meant I was still alive.

The need to grieve allows the process of 'letting go' to begin properly. It is important for the place of resolution to be reached and to know that your child is at rest. Within the grieving is often the unspoken question: 'Did my child suffer pain because of me?' A response of gentle honesty is important. To acknowledge that it is known that babies in the womb feel pain is better than a trite 'no' but what also needs to be heard is that now the child is in a place of no pain.

At this stage many who perhaps have no obvious Church commitment begin to ask: 'Where does God fit in?' To know that a life which was unfulfilled here on earth can find fulfilment in heaven, to know that a child is loved and cared for, to know that one day there can be a re-uniting of mother and child: these are not trite panaceas but part of the Christian hope.

Forgiveness

The problem of forgiveness is not exclusive to women who have had abortions! As with anger, it can often be part of the self-punishment to withhold oneself from experiencing forgiveness.

The process of forgiveness includes believing that:

- you can be forgiven, that abortion is not the unforgivable sin but a forgivable one;

- God can forgive and that the promise of absolution in Scripture is trustworthy;

- the unborn child can forgive you;

- you can forgive yourself.

Forgiveness is a process that needs to be worked at, it needs to be seen in the context of sorting out blame. The question needs to be asked: 'What am I responsible for and what are others responsible for?'

As Christians we know that Jesus' love goes hand-in-hand with self-forgiveness. With this love, the woman hurt by abortion can make changes in her life; she can discard her old self-image and take on a new one. With the courage of love, she can dare to forgive herself. There is a challenge for us in the Church to communicate this reality.

As women hurt by abortion begin to voice their pain and trauma, the crippling effects can begin to dissipate and a moving on can begin.

As women hurt by abortion begin to voice their pain and trauma, the crippling effects can begin to dissipate and a moving on can begin.

As the months went on I found that it was less the agony of my loss that dominated my thoughts and more the cherishing of my child.

Jane told me one day this will seem different and that there was hope. Even though she spoke from experience, part of me couldn't dare to believe her. I know now she was right.

Bridging the gap
There are countless stories of women confronting their abortion experience and finding healing and peace and discovering that they are not condemned to this pain for ever. How can Christians effectively bridge the gap and show women the way to the source of healing – to God? Through experience we have discovered that it is important to:

- pray that for the women the memories will begin to surface and an end to the suffering will be seen;
- pray for the work of BVA which is frequently costly, and that the counsellors themselves will be strengthened;
- pray for the voice of the child. In our churches we need to hear people speaking out and clearly stating that abortion is wrong.

If you are involved with a woman who has had an abortion:

- be prepared to stand alongside and to share her pain;
- be patient: the healing process is not instant!
- allow the child to become real. Encourage the naming of the child. This is often important as a means of committing the child to God's care;
- don't be afraid to confront the reality of what has happened: a child died.

Conclusion
One of the most effective voices in the pro-life cause comes from the women who have suffered the trauma of abortion and who can say: 'There are two victims in every abortion, the child and the woman'. I know how much this costs because I have done it. I and many others know what abortion does to women's lives, but we also know that from the darkness there really does come light! I have been asked frequently; 'How can you be pro-life

I have been asked frequently; 'How can you be pro-life when you've had an abortion?' The question I ask is: 'How can I not be after an abortion?'

when you've had an abortion?' The question I ask is: 'How can I not be after an abortion?'

> ... because of the tender mercy of our God,
> by which the rising sun will come to us from heaven
> to shine on those living in darkness
> and in the shadow of death,
> to guide our feet into the path of peace.
> *Luke 1:78–79*

This chapter has only been written with the help of those women who have allowed their voices to be heard and I am grateful to them for allowing me to quote them. It is also important to recognise that BVA exists because of SPUC's commitment. They have over the years kept faith in us all and enabled us to move on and develop.

Within BVA there has been much pain and suffering but there has also been much love and care. As a group we recognise that there can be purpose from the destruction we have all experienced.

British Victims of Abortion can be contacted at:

BVA
P.O. Box 91
Glasgow G1 2DB
Tel: 0229 870043, 041 226 5407 or 0908 262855.

CHAPTER TEN

Christian responsibility in public affairs

You are the light of the world. A city on a hill cannot be hidden.
Matthew 5:14

Changing the law means involvement in the political process.

If the Christian in Britain today is concerned to protect unborn children, then inevitably this will mean calling for a change in the law. Changing the law means involvement in the political process. Is this a legitimate arena for Christian involvement?

'The Great Reversal'

Recent years have seen a considerable change in evangelical thinking on the legitimacy of political involvement. In the 1960s and 1970s considerable debate took place among evangelicals on the subject, and in 1974 the Lausanne Congress (attended by some 2,700 people from around the world) recognised in its Covenant that 'socio-political involvement' was part of our Christian duty. During this time, the late Dr Francis Schaeffer was challenging Christians to apply Christian truth in every area of life. His influence reached a peak in the late 1970s with the publication of *Whatever Happened to the Human Race?* (which he co-authored with Dr C. Everett Koop) and the accompanying films. Before this, however, evangelical social and political involvement had often been discouraged, being considered to be unholy, unscriptural and a sign of willingness to compromise that was incompatible with true Christian discipleship.

Why was this so? The nineteenth century had seen evangelical Christians like Lord Shaftesbury, William Wilberforce and many others at the forefront of political life. The Rev. Dr John Stott in *Issues Facing Christians Today* gives five reasons for what is commonly known as 'The Great Reversal' – the retreat of evangelical Christians from the political arena.[1]

First, he states, there was 'a reaction against theological liberalism'. Since its emergence in the mid-nineteenth century theological liberalism had been gaining ground, particularly in theological education. In the face of doubts concerning the deity of Christ and the authority of the Bible, evangelicals were more concerned with maintaining a clear orthodox voice on these vital theological questions than with involvement in social action.

Second, Stott maintains that 'evangelicals reacted against the so-called "social gospel"'. Those who espoused the 'social gospel' believed the work of the Church to be in transforming society rather than in calling for individual conversion. This, to evangelicals, denied the priority of the Great Commission to 'go and make disciples of all nations' (Matthew 28:19) and as such was to be rejected. So, the close relationship between evangelism and social action was severed. The debate was framed in terms of *either* evangelism *or* social action.

Only months before his death Francis Schaeffer was one of the speakers at the 1983 SPUC rally in Hyde Park, 'A Call to Humanity'.

Third, the influence of the First World War was considerable. It exposed the evil and sickness that was at work in the world. It revealed the wickedness of the human heart. The widespread social upheaval and unprecedented loss of human life produced a pessimism that led Christians to look above to their true home – heaven. Individual conversion was paramount in an evil world and any hope of transforming it was lost. The political world was seen as being all too much a part of the fallen world.

Fourth, the pre-millennial scheme was widely proclaimed. This doctrine espoused the idea that the present world was evil and beyond redemption. There was no hope of making a better world since it would continue to deteriorate until Jesus came to reign on earth again. There was no point in social action.

The fifth reason, Stott believes, was the spread of evangelicalism among the middle classes which led to an over-identification of their values with Christianity.

Public v. Private

One reason for this 'Great Reversal' not highlighted by Stott was the division between public and private in common thinking. With the dawn of the Age of Reason, or the Enlightenment, in the mid-eighteenth century, came the belief that some things had public value, for example facts, as in scientific or mathematical facts, and other things had only private value, for example faith, beliefs or values. Religious belief of whatever type was relegated to the 'private' category.

This belief gradually infiltrated the churches, which lacked the conviction to challenge such false divisions. The accepted role of the Church in this system of belief was to concentrate on the individual and remain on the margins of public debate and

The political world was seen as being all too much a part of the fallen world.

involvement. There were, of course, notable exceptions, particularly in nineteenth-century Britain following the Evangelical Revival, but that was not enough to challenge this division of public and private which was carried along on the tide of rationalism.

These, then, are the ideas that shaped the 'Great Reversal'. Recent thinking about Christian political and social responsibility has, however, taken into account scriptural emphases that challenge evangelicals to reassess their witness in the arena of public affairs, and to follow their nineteenth-century forebears in making a determined contribution in this area.

Stewardship

First there has come a new awareness of the doctrine of stewardship. This is the belief that human beings are stewards of God's world, in his place to care for and manage his world. They key doctrine is rooted in the Creation narrative in the first two chapters of Genesis:

> Then God said, 'Let us make man in our image, in our likeness, and let them rule over the fish of the sea and the birds of the air, over the livestock, over all the earth, and over all the creatures that move along the ground'.
>
> *Genesis 1:26*

Man (which in this context denotes human beings) is made in the image of God, the pinnacle of creation, but with a special role to play in the world God has brought into being. He is given great privileges and great responsibilities. He is to 'rule ... over all the earth'. Men and women together are to be God's vicegerents in this world. However, this does not give human beings *carte-blanche* to treat the world destructively. Human beings are accountable to the One who made them — Almighty God.

Adam's rule over the earth is symbolised by his naming of the animals.

Chapter 2 of Genesis gives a picture of man and God in a dynamic relationship. God places Adam in the Garden of Eden and guides him in the responsibilities he is to assume. For example, Adam's rule over the earth is symbolised by his naming of the animals. However, God places clear limits on man's rule. Adam is not to eat of the tree of the knowledge of good and evil. When that limit is crossed the relationship of the Creator and the created changes completely and only in Jesus Christ can that relationship be restored.

What relevance does the doctrine of stewardship have for a discussion of Christian political responsibility? The key surely lies in the concept of ruling the earth. It is clear, from the naming of the animals, that man is to organise his world. It is also clear that man is to use the earth for his good – for food, clothing and shelter. But does this role as ruler apply solely to man's dealings with the natural world? Does it have anything to say about the organisation of human society, which is, in fact, politics? This is a modern problem. In the biblical societies, community life was relatively simple compared with that of modern nation-states. Their communities were based on agriculture and, when they began to be more complex, political responsibility was in the hands of the few who were appointed by God. There was no division between Church and State. Democracy is a relatively new phenomenon!

God's command to man was to rule over the earth and 'all the creatures that move along the ground'. It would be inconsistent for God to give man authority over the natural world but not over the human world. Indeed we have to ask, can the two worlds be separated? Scripturally the created order is seen as a whole, under God and sustained by his grace and power. Therefore, the ordering, organisation and management of human societies – politics – must be seen as part of man's role as steward of God's world. Indeed it is absolutely necessary that such political organisation take place, otherwise chaos quickly ensues and, as in the days when Israel had no king, everyone does as he sees fit (Judges 21:25).

Politics must be seen as part of man's role as steward of God's world.

The second great commandment

Jesus Christ gave his followers two great commandments, which are to form the basis of their lives. They are:

> 'Love the Lord your God with all your heart and with all your soul and with all your mind.' This is the first and greatest commandment. And the second is like it: 'Love your neighbour as yourself'.
>
> *Matthew 22: 37–39*

It is the application of the second great commandment that relates to our discussion of Christian political responsibility. Traditionally, this has been rightly applied to 'good works' – or philanthropic deeds for the good of others. However, it has wider application in modern democratic societies. Public policies impinge daily on the lives of millions, for good or ill, and policies are created, managed and changed by politicians. Therefore, to love and care for our neighbours as Christ commanded, it is essential that Christians be involved in the decision-making processes of society. This is as much a way of 'loving your neighbour' as any good work done for a particular individual.

If a law disadvantages a particular group it is not sufficient to help afflicted individuals while leaving the unjust structure in place. We must also strive to change the unjust law. When a tap has been left running we do not just mop up the overflow; the important thing is to turn off the tap. Changing an unjust law is like turning off that tap.

When a tap has been left running we do not just mop up the overflow; the important thing is to turn off the tap.

Salt and light

A further biblical picture that can inform this discussion is that of God's people being the salt of the earth and the light of the world (Matthew 5:13–16). Salt cannot do its work if it is in the salt cellar. It has to be combined with food both to give flavour and to preserve. Jesus describes Christians in this way. They are not to lose their saltiness but to have a good and challenging effect upon those around them.

Christians are also the 'light of the world'. What good will a light do if it is under a bowl? To give light where needed it has to be displayed prominently. Jesus' conclusion is 'let your light shine before men, that they may see your good deeds and praise your Father in heaven' (Matthew 5:16). The political arena needs a great deal of salt and light. Christians need to be working in the midst of public life bringing the flavour and light of God into a dark world.

Judgement and its basis

When Jesus is teaching his disciples about his own Second Coming (Matthew 25) he introduces two concepts which directly impinge upon this subject of political responsibility. The first is judgement. When Jesus speaks of the separation of the sheep and the goats he says that:

> All the nations will be gathered before him, and he will separate the people from one another as a shepherd separates the sheep from the goats.
>
> *Matthew 25:32*

There will be judgement for the nations. The second concept is contained in the criteria for judgement which Jesus goes on to elucidate. The criteria will be whether the hungry were fed, the stranger welcomed, the prisoner visited or the sick cared for. This has direct implications for public policy. Does public policy reflect these all-important biblical criteria?

Government and God

A further strong reason why Christians should be involved in political structures is that the Bible has a high view of government. This is most clearly set out in Romans 13:1–7. Here Paul establishes that God is sovereign and it is he who gives authority to the earthly leaders. He can say categorically that 'The authorities that exist have been established by God', and that 'there is no authority except that which God has established'.

It is interesting that he can state this despite having been constantly at odds with the Roman authorities because of his preaching of the Gospel. Paul urges his followers to be law-abiding and respectful of authority. Some have argued that this is all that Paul requires of believers and that personal involvement in such government is therefore unnecessary. However, Paul could hardly exhort his followers to become personally involved in a system of government that admitted no such outside influence. In the first century AD citizens of the Roman Empire had few of the opportunities which present themselves

St. Paul respected the temporal authority of the Roman Empire. William Hogarth depicted him appearing before Felix.

to those living in twentieth-century democracies!

Paul also describes the role of the governing authorities. They are to punish the wrongdoer and are to govern financially through taxes. They are to keep order in the community through being the agent of punishment.

Perhaps the greatest indication of Paul's high view of government is the fact that he calls government officials 'God's servants'. Public officials are referred to in this way three times in seven verses. It is most unlikely that he is referring to Christians in public service as he has already referred to all authority as being from God whether Christian or not. Paul also regards himself as God's servant. Therefore, he is referring to those in government as being in God's service just as he is serving God as an apostle.

> *Perhaps the greatest indication of Paul's high view of government is the fact that he calls government officials 'God's servants'.*

Paul exhorts Timothy to urge his churches to pray 'for kings and all those in authority' (1 Timothy 2:1–2). It would be inconsistent to argue that Christians should pray for their government but, where the opportunity exists, refuse to take part in it. In the light of this and Paul's teaching on the role of government in Romans 13 it is not unreasonable to deduce that, if the opportunities for involvement in the political process which we take for granted had existed in the days of the Roman Empire, Paul would have urged Christians to be at the heart of government.

In his skirmish with the Pharisees Jesus recognised and endorsed the right of government to impose taxation (Matthew 22:15–21). In doing so he legitimised the limited role of governments in their citizens' lives. He also set limits by saying that those same citizens must be free to give to God what is due to him.

God's people in power

Two Old Testament characters are crucial to the consideration of this issue: Joseph and Daniel. Both were used by God in high-ranking positions of political responsibility in foreign nations. Joseph's foresight and shrewd management saved Egypt from famine and ruin. Daniel was appointed as a top administrator in Babylon. It is said of him that:

> . . . the administrators and the satraps tried to find grounds for charges against Daniel in his conduct of government affairs, but they were unable to do so. They could find no corruption in him, because he was trustworthy and neither corrupt nor negligent.
>
> *Daniel 6:4*

Both Joseph and Daniel faced situations in which compromise was tempting, but neither succumbed. The danger of compromise is a common concern for Christians looking at the political arena. Is compromise inevitable? First, it is necessary to define what is meant by compromise. Not all compromise is bad. Indeed in a nation-state comprising millions of individuals some compromise is inevitable. Everyone has to compromise in order to live in a community, whether it be in a family, work-place or nation.

However, this is completely different from compromise of a person's moral principles. Both Joseph and Daniel refused to compromise their moral standards. Joseph refused the advances of Potiphar's wife and Daniel refused to stop praying to Israel's

God. It was difficult for them but God gave them the necessary strength. They serve as an example to others.

In the modern context an example of political compromise concerns the form of Bills that have been presented to Parliament to amend the 1967 Abortion Act. Parliamentarians have never presented Bills which would make abortion illegal in all cases except where the mother's life is in danger. There has been confusion over this tactic among many Christians. It is clear that if a Bill to outlaw abortion completely – an 'absolutist' Bill – were presented, it would attract so little support that it would be lost. However, a Bill which contained restrictions on abortion would save some lives if it were passed. What is the Christian to do? To try to stop abortion completely and get nowhere or try to stop some and have a greater chance of success in Parliament? It is, of course, the latter course of action that is the most expedient and this is the nature of political compromise.

A further encouragement for Christians in politics is found in Jesus' high-priestly prayer in which he prays for his disciples and all believers in the ages to come: 'Holy Father, protect them by the power of your name' (John 17:11), and later: 'My prayer is not that you take them out of the world but that you protect them from the evil one' (John 17:15). Jesus' followers are not going to be taken out of the world but are to be protected while they work within it in all spheres of life.

The Christian contribution

What insight does the Christian faith have to contribute to public policy and political thought? Of primary importance is the belief in the ultimate value of human life. This affects policy on a number of levels. For example, the criminal law should be framed and implemented to ensure that people are valued above property.

Above all, the Christian ethos informs law on abortion, human embryo experimentation and euthanasia. This reflects the frequently repeated biblical injunction to care for the widow and the orphan, who represent in this context the weak and vulnerable. As unborn children are among the most vulnerable members of modern society, their protection should be the first priority of a government based on Christian principles.

Then there is the knowledge that life has a spiritual element which needs to be respected in public affairs. Together with this is the Christian's prophetic role in declaring that we are accountable to Almighty God. We are not our own masters.

As unborn children are among the most vulnerable members of modern society, their protection should be the first priority of a government based on Christian principles.

A lobby of Parliament in defence of the unborn child.

Impose or influence?

Should we expect to pass laws that reflect Christian values in a pluralist society, many of whose members do not subscribe to the Christian faith? Is this attempting to impose our values on others?

There is a great difference between imposing unwanted restrictions on others and trying to influence public debate. To impose is clearly undesirable and in democratic societies there are checks to prevent this happening. Parliaments are democratically elected and will have some relation to the spread of views in the community of the nation.

However, imposing Christian ethics on an unwilling nation is completely different from participating in public debate on subjects such as abortion and other life issues on which Christians have a special contribution to make. Christians may not win all they want, they may gain nothing, but it is essential to use the opportunity to plead for the rights of the weak and disadvantaged. To fail to do so is to fail in our responsibility as stewards.

Evangelism *v.* social action?

Is there a conflict between evangelism and social action?

The Church is called first and foremost to 'go and make disciples of all nations' (Matthew 28:19). Therefore the Church's first priority is to preach the good news of Jesus Christ. However, Jesus did not leave a method but a command. The discovery of the means and methods of proclaiming the good news is left to each generation. What every generation has found is that showing love and care to the needy and oppressed is vital in this task. Social action is an essential part of evangelism. This is not surprising since Jesus himself linked goods works or social action with the adoption of faith:

Social action is an essential part of evangelism.

> . . . let your light shine before men, that they may see your good deeds and praise your Father in heaven.
>
> *Matthew 5:16*

Likewise in the letter of James, faith and deeds are linked:

> Suppose a brother or sister is without clothes and daily food. If one of you says to him, 'Go, I wish you well; keep warm and well fed,' but does nothing about his physical needs, what good is it? In the same way, faith by itself, if it is not accompanied by action, is dead.
>
> *James 2:15–17*

It would seem, then, that evangelism and social action are inextricably linked in the Christian faith. It is all part of loving our neighbour. It must be remembered, however, that motives are vital. Christians must constantly ask themselves when involved in social or political action, 'Why am I doing this?' The motive must never be self-promotion but Christ-promotion. Christians are to engage in social or political action for the love of their neighbour and in the hope that by doing so they may point non-believers to Jesus Christ himself.

The 'single issue' argument

To conclude, then, there is a strong case for political involvement on the part of Christians. Not to be involved in this area is to neglect a basic Christian responsibility. For many, this

involvement will not mean standing for political office but will be at the level of voting. Deciding how to vote is a microcosm of all political decisions – it will be a compromise. However, certain key principles are crucial in making that decision. The first must be to ask how candidates stand on the issues of human life – abortion, infanticide and euthanasia. Will they commit themselves, if elected to Parliament, to voting for the protection of human life at all stages? If not, they can hardly be considered suitable candidates for political office, no matter how appealing their other policies may be. If Christians can do nothing else, they can use their vote and make it count for the unborn.

It may be argued by some Christians that it is wrong for Christians to vote on a single issue only: the sanctity of human life.

Of course, it is true that there are many issues – social issues and political issues – about which the Christian must be concerned: these include, to name but a few, homelessness, education, the health service, unemployment and so on. Clearly,

Lyndon Bowring of CARE and Nigel Cameron join marchers protesting against abortion.

the sanctity of life is not the only issue facing the Christian voter as he goes to the polling booth.

However, as Christians, we are bound to ask the following question: is it morally right to vote for a politician who believes in legislation which permits the killing of our fellow human beings? Supposing we were living in a society in which it was lawful to kill Jews or Muslims or Christians? Would it not be morally wrong to vote for politicans who believed in such legislation? Whatever their merits, this would render such people unfit to hold office.

The sanctity of life should not be regarded as a 'single issue' but as a disqualifying issue.

The sanctity of life, therefore, should not be regarded as a 'single issue' but as a *disqualifying issue*. Just as it is inconceivable that a Christian could, in justice, vote for a politician who believed in killing one's *born* neighbours, so it is inconceivable that a Christian could, in justice, vote for a politician who believes in killing his *unborn* neighbours. There may be other disqualifying issues for the Christian voter but this one is surely paramount since it is the condition of all others. One cannot exercise the right to work without enjoying the right to life, for example.

Scripture itself judges political leaders by how well they uphold God's law rather than by their skill or success as politicians. Thus Herod the Great, who gained that title for his remarkable astuteness and administrative achievements, is chiefly noted in the Bible for his slaughter of innocent children in response to the birth of Christ (Matt. 2:16–18). In the Old Testament the long and glittering career of Jeroboam the Second merits just seven verses of 2 Kings and is summarised in the familiar words: 'He did evil in the eyes of the Lord' (2 Kings 14:24). Other able but ungodly leaders are assessed in a similar way. As Christians in the modern world we have the right and the duty to judge the views and actions of politicians by the eternal standards of God's laws.

The reality is that in the end it is only this that will make the difference. As Francis Schaeffer and C. Everett Koop wrote in *Whatever Happened to the Human Race?*:

Acknowledging Christ's Lordship and placing ourselves under what is taught in the whole Bible includes thinking and acting as citizens in relation to our government and its laws.[2]

CHAPTER ELEVEN

Our guilty silence

But if the watchman sees the sword coming and does not blow the trumpet to
warn the people and the sword comes and takes the life of one of them, that
man will be taken away because of his sin, but I will hold the watchman
accountable for his blood.
Ezekiel 33:6

How can we explain the failure of the Church to respond to the abuse and destruction of unborn children? Undoubtedly the Church has failed, even though many Christians have taken a stand and support for the pro-life organisations is largely Christian. For when the response of the Church as a whole is measured against the enormity of what has happened in our midst, it is utterly incongruous. An occasional, circumspect resolution,[1] reports that leave the value of human life in question,[2] lukewarm support for attempts to amend the law – these are hardly an adequate response to the deliberate killing of nearly four million children.

For most of the time the subject is simply not mentioned in Christian circles. This is as true of evangelicals as of others. In its context, this silence is as remarkable as the strange silence of the Church in Germany during the atrocities of the Nazi era.

A number of explanations may account for this silence.

This silence is as remarkable as the strange silence of the Church in Germany during the atrocities of the Nazi era.

Ignorance

Without doubt, the British population remains uninformed about the facts of abortion and the related threats to human life. The mass media, and particularly the broadcast media, play down or do not report what is happening,[3] do not reveal the horrific violence suffered by the victims of abortion, and consistently favour the proponents of abortion in discussion of the issue. The resulting impression is that abortion is an acceptable – if distasteful – feature of everyday life, of marginal concern except for those with a special interest.[4]

Christians who rely on the mass media for their information will remain as unaware of the seriousness of what is happening as the public at large. And yet, as we saw in Chapter 10, we

have a clear duty to seek to be informed about the results of laws passed by people we have elected, about medical operations and research paid for with our taxes, about the evil that is being done to our neighbour. 'We did not know' is a thin excuse (Proverbs 24:12).

Lack of conviction

Most people feel a natural revulsion at the practices of abortion and embryo experimentation, especially when they understand what these involve. Not many Christians would wish to be advocates of these practices; however, a number of people have put forward arguments that attempt to give a Christian justification for allowing them. We have considered some of these arguments in Chapter 3. Those who remain convinced that abortion can be justified may, of course, still speak out against its current widespread use, but they are much less likely to do so. Moreover, they set themselves against the view of Christians through the ages (see Chapter 1), against the commandments of God to treat life as sacred, and against the uniform witness of Scripture that every human life is of value in God's eyes.

More telling for many are the 'hard cases', and these have been given special consideration in Chapters 4 and 8. Hard cases (usually hypothetical ones) are often used by the advocates of abortion, experimentation and euthanasia to try and silence the pro-life voice. We must be clear in our minds that we cannot simply ignore the fact that every life, however apparently disadvantaged, is sacred. It cannot be right to solve our problems by killing an innocent party. In cases such as pregnancy resulting from rape, the unborn child is an innocent party. Christians should not be ashamed to point this out.

Concern about the pro-life 'agenda'

One of the commonest misapprehensions about the pro-life message is that it is intimately bound up with some programme or other. The media frequently make this implication, whether it is that pro-lifers are right-wing, or women-haters, or 'catholic'. These ideas are often deployed to deter people from thinking seriously about the issues.

None of the major parties in Britain has an acceptable policy of protecting unborn life.

So far as party politics are concerned, it must be pointed out that none of the major parties in Britain has an acceptable policy of protecting unborn life.[5] At the same time, pro-life members – including MPs – of all parties have taken a strong stand on behalf of unborn children, sometimes at great personal cost.

Any political party will be enriched by the contribution of

Christian members. What is required is that Christians should understand clearly that the sanctity of life is a first principle which must underpin any social programme; and those who have a political allegiance must strive to establish this basis within their parties.

It is a sad fact that 'abortion rights' have featured prominently in much of the campaigning of feminists in this century and in earlier times. Some feminists have, however, seen the inherent contradiction in asserting one's rights by trampling over someone else's.[6]

It is tragic that the interests of mothers and their babies should be divided in this way. The testimonies in Chapter 9 show that women are victims of abortion too. To be pro-life is by no means to be anti-women; it is to recognise the dignity of both mother and child. The wisdom of God has bound their lives together: to harm one is to harm both, to care for one is to care for both.

To be pro-life is by no means to be anti-women; it is to recognise the dignity of both mother and child.

Pro-life organisations are supported by people with a wide range of religious beliefs, including atheists. Roman Catholics, partly because of the official teaching of their church, have played a large part in the development of pro-life work, but by no means to the exclusion of others. In Northern Ireland, for example, evangelicals have played a key role in the resistance to legalising abortion.

SPUC Evangelicals has been formed in the conviction that those who believe and obey God's word must resist the gross violation of human life that is at present tolerated in our society. It provides fellowship and mutual support for Christians sharing this conviction, and practical means of working to defend unborn children along with others who respect human life.[7]

Priorities

There are many demands on the time and energy of modern Christians. We are rightly aware of many needs and good causes that we could support to serve Christ in a fallen world. It is understandable if sometimes the plight of unborn children is seen as just one cause among many, and passed over in favour of something that is apparently more obvious or urgent. Once again, lack of information is a problem here, for Christians who were properly informed about what is happening to unborn children would be much more eager to try to help them.

It is more important, however, that we realise that this is not 'just another cause'; the pro-life campaign is maintaining a fundamental Christian position that human life is sacred. This position is now being directly challenged by the legalisation of

abortion and embryo experimentation. Once the sanctity of life is denied then the value of every human life is in question. The growing pressure for euthanasia is witness to this. It is essential, therefore, to maintain the sanctity of life as a first priority. If we do not, we will not have an adequate basis for any other 'cause' that might commend itself. For example, if we are prepared to allow people to be killed because they are regarded as 'unwanted', why should it matter to us if others suffer from famine, homelessness or lack of education?

Similarly, the very preaching of the Gospel requires a pro-life position. The Gospel's urgency should not be used as a reason to evade the issue of the sanctity of life. We wish to affirm the priority of preaching the message of salvation; however, this message includes the assurance that people are loved by God out of his sheer grace, and this love, of course, puts a value on human life that can only be met by the price of Christ's death (1 John 4:10). To deny the sanctity of human life is to deny this central truth of the Gospel message. It is impossible to preach the Gospel with integrity unless one takes a pro-life stand.

Sir Bernard Braine – now Lord Braine of Wheatley – was for many years the leader of the All Party Parliamentary Pro-Life Group.

Failure of leadership
Another reason for the silence of Christians is the failure of

The sanctity of human life is low on the agenda of the Church as well as the world.

Christian leaders to make a stand. This is true both of national leadership within the churches, and of the lead given to local congregations by their pastors. Leaders do take a stand on issues of the day, sometimes bravely, sometimes with the comparative ease of sharing in the condemnation of something that is universally deplored. But a leader who speaks up clearly and uncompromisingly against the outrageous treatment of unborn children is a rarity. Sad to say, the most basic of all issues, the sanctity of human life, is low on the agenda of the Church as well as the world.

There are various reasons why it is particularly hard for Church leaders to speak out on this issue, and we deal with some of them below. However, leaders must recognise that until they give a clear lead in this matter, those in their care will be perplexed and hesitant in responding to the plight of unborn children.

> Again, if the trumpet does not sound a clear call, who will get ready for battle?
>
> *1 Cor. 14:8*

This is part of their vocation as leaders, even though it may be difficult, uncomfortable or unpopular.

False compassion

So widespread has abortion become that nearly all congregations in Britain will include people who either have had an abortion or have close family members who have had one. Sensitive Christians, moved by the plight of unborn children, may remain silent about abortion out of concern for those whom they know to have had one. Those who preach will be particularly aware of this problem if they tackle the subject in sermons.

Getting the Church to face this issue needs care and courage, but face it we must. There can be no avoiding it in the complacent hope that matters will simply resolve themselves. If we do that, more and more children – including children of Church members – will be killed, because no one said anything. More and more women – including Church members – will join the ranks of grieving mothers, because no one gave them the guidance they needed. The burden of guilt, anger and confusion, so clearly described in Chapter 9, will grow more and more intractable until we honestly admit the truth.

Those who fear the pastoral consequences of raising the question of abortion in their churches should take encourage-

IN MEMORY OF
3,000,000
CHILDREN
KILLED BY ABORTION
SINCE
1967

ment from the testimony of Chapter 9.[8] The general experience of ministers who do give a clear pro-life lead to their congregation is that it is enormously appreciated. In particular, people who may have been wrestling for years with their own inner turmoil welcome the opportunity at last to seek help and Christ's forgiveness. This is true compassion.

Complicity

We should also realise that people are involved with abortion in different ways. There are family members who have applied pressure, or failed to give help. There are professionals who have played a part in some way. In particular, we must realise that every single one of the millions of children who have been legally aborted in this country has been killed by a doctor, working within our medical profession. The 1967 Abortion Act gives a right to doctors, nurses and medical staff to refuse to take part in abortion procedures; sadly, not many in the medical profession have availed themselves of that right.[9] To the tally of abortion victims must also be added now the victims of embryo experiments and the newborn handicapped who have been starved to death under medical supervision.

We are facing an enormous burden of guilt and there are Church members who share in it.

Again we are facing an enormous burden of guilt, and again there are Church members who share in it. We cannot pretend that Christians – doctors and others – have not been involved: they have. We cannot pretend that somehow, because Christians are involved, it must be all right: it is not. Raising the subject of unborn children in the Church will inevitably have implications for those in the Church who have an involvement with abortion. This may discourage us. But much of what was written about false compassion applies here also. We may be sure that, where there is true repentance and faith in Christ, his forgiveness can be found:

> But if anybody does sin, we have one who speaks to the Father in our defence – Jesus Christ, the Righteous One. He is the atoning sacrifice for our sins.
>
> *1 John 2:1–2*

These things come from speaking the truth, not from remaining silent.

Fear of how we will be seen

Moral issues are often very complex, so that an informed opinion may require considerable knowledge and careful thought. The danger is that such issues will then be seen as chiefly matters of opinion and discussion, and the moral imperative to act will be lost.

We have no wish to stifle debate; indeed this book is intended to provide information and biblical insights which will help Christians understand the issues we are dealing with more fully. But it is not sufficient that we should engage in interesting discussion: in the end, God requires us to act on his word.

Christians have fought against slavery, racism, torture and many other evils. In each case there were opposing points of view to take into account, but the examination of the issue would have been a meaningless exercise without the action that followed. Similarly, we will one day have to answer to God, not on whether we debated 'the abortion issue', but on whether we acted to protect unborn children made in his image.

We will one day have to answer to God on whether we acted to protect unborn children.

This exposes us and we feel vulnerable. Those who stand uncompromisingly for life are not gladly received. We fear what people will think of us. We are insisting on the sanctity of life in all circumstances, in a world where moral absolutes are no longer acceptable and all is relative. We are portrayed as fascists, restricting people's freedoms, whereas it is in fact the pro-abortionists who adopt the essentially fascist position of creating a graduated scale of human rights, particularly in relation to the right to life of handicapped people. We are denounced as heretics, offending against the new orthodoxy that individual freedom of choice is not only good but the final arbiter of all questions. Worst of all, we are condemned for making people feel guilty and for taking a judgemental stance, contrary to Scripture (Matthew 7:1–2).

And all this silences the Christian.

Each one of us must make a choice either to join the conspiracy of silence, or to speak out, uncomfortable though that may be. It is a question of whom we obey: 'Judge for yourselves whether it is right in God's sight to obey you rather than God' said Peter and John to those who would have silenced them (Acts 4:19).

The slaughter still goes on. While it does, those who love God's justice and mercy, who have compassion in their hearts and are led by his Spirit, will choose to hear what he says and obey God:

> Speak up for those who cannot speak for themselves,
> for the rights of all who are destitute.
> Speak up and judge fairly;
> defend the rights of the poor and needy.
>
> *Proverbs 31:8–9*

When Herod realised that he had been outwitted by the Magi, he was furious, and he gave orders to kill all the boys in Bethlehem and its vicinity who were two years old and under, in accordance with the time he had learned from the Magi. Then what was said through the prophet Jeremiah was fulfilled:

'A voice is heard in Ramah,
weeping and great mourning,
Rachel weeping for her children
and refusing to be comforted,
because they are no more.'

Matthew 2:16–18

SPUC Evangelicals

SPUC Evangelicals (a division of the Society for the Protection of Unborn Children) was formed in 1991. It is a member organisation of the Evangelical Alliance.

Aims

1   To promote the biblical understanding of the sanctity of human life, as it is set out in the Basis of Action.
2   To work with churches, societies and other bodies having an Evangelical presence so that they may fulfil their task of defending unborn children.
3   To assist individual Christians in taking a pro-life stand.

Basis of Action

In accordance with the witness of Scripture, we believe:

1   That God made man in his own image.
2   That the Son of God became flesh in the womb of his mother, so sharing our humanity from the time of conception.
3   That every human life from conception to death, without exception, therefore has an intrinsic dignity and is to be respected.
4   That the widespread abuse and destruction of unborn children therefore constitute a flagrant offence against almighty God.
5   That obedience to God's Word and compassion for the victims of this offence require Christians to speak out against the abuse and destruction of unborn children and to seek their protection.

Membership is open to members of SPUC who are in agreement with the Basis of Action and wish to pursue the Aims.

Further information can be obtained by writing to:

SPUC Evangelicals
7 Tufton Street
London SW1P 3QN
Tel: 071 222 5845

Bibliography

GENERAL

Johnston, Raymond, *Caring and Campaigning*, Marshall Pickering (1990), ISBN 0-551-01879-8.

Newbiggin, Lesslie, *Foolishness to the Greeks*, SPCK (1986), ISBN 0-281-04232-2.

Stott, Rev. Dr John, *Issues Facing Christians Today*, Marshall Pickering (1984), ISBN 0-551-01879-8.

ABORTION

Cameron, Nigel M. de S. and Sims, Pamela F., *Abortion: The Crisis in Morals and Medicine*, Inter-Varsity Press (1986), ISBN 0-85110-447-0.

Channer, J.H. (Ed.) *Abortion and the Sanctity of Human Life*, Paternoster Press Exeter (1985), ISBN 0-85364-417-9.

Koop, C. Everett, M.D., *The Right to Live, The Right to Die*, Tyndale House Publishers, Wheaton Illinois (1980), ISBN 0-8423 5593-6.

• LaGard Smith, F., *When Choice Becomes God*, Harvest House, Eugene, Oregon (1990), ISBN 0-89081-828-2 (Price: £5.50).

O'Donovan, Oliver, *The Christian and the Unborn Child*, Grove Books, Bramcote (2nd ed., 1975), ISBN 0-901710-67-9.

• Powell, John, *Abortion: The Silent Holocaust*, Argus Communications, Texas (1981), ISBN 0-89505-063-3 (Price: £3.95).

Riols, Noreen, *Abortion: a woman's birthright?* Hodder & Stoughton, London (1986), ISBN 0-340-39135-9.

Schaeffer, Francis and Koop, C. Everett, M.D., *Whatever Happened to the Human Race?* Marshall Morgan and Scott, (1980), ISBN 0-551-00870-9.

Swindoll, Charles R., *Sanctity of Life: The Inescapable Issue*, Word (UK) Ltd, Milton Keynes (1990), ISBN 0-85009-346-5.

Wenham, Dr Gordon and White, Dr Richard, *Abortion: The biblical and medical challenges*, CARE Trust, London (1983).

- Whelan, Robert (ed.) *Legal Abortion Examined: 21 Years of Abortion Statistics*, SPUC Educational Research Trust, London (1992), ISBN 0-946680-37-X (Price: £5.95).

- White, Dr Margaret, *Two Million Silent Killings*, Marshall Pickering (1987), ISBN 0-551-01402-4 (Price: £5.95).

- Willke, Dr and Mrs J. C., *Abortion: Questions and Answers*, Hayes Publishing Company, Cincinatti (1985), ISBN 0-910728-20-8 (Price: £3.50).

- Winter, Dr Richard, *Choose Life: A Christian Perspective on Abortion and Embryo Experiments*, Marshall Pickering, Basingstoke (1988), ISBN 0-551-01576-4.

MEDICAL ETHICS

Cameron, Nigel M. de S. (ed.), *Ethics and Medicine: A Christian perspective on issues in bioethics*, Journal, appears thrice yearly, ISSN: 0266-688X, 16pp. and cover. Details of subscription from Centre for Bioethics and Public Policy, 58 Hanover Gardens, London SE11 5TN.

Cameron, Nigel M. de S. (ed.), *Embryos and Ethics*, Rutherford House Books, Edinburgh (1987), ISBN 0-946068-22-4 but now available through the Centre for Bioethics and Public Policy, address as above.

Wilkinson, John, *Christian Ethics in Healthcare*, Handsel Press (1988).

EMBRYOLOGY AND FETOLOGY

- Chargaff, Prof. E., Lejeune, Prof. J., McLean, Dr J., *Upholding Human Dignity: Ethical Alternatives to Human Embryo Research*, Parliamentary Medical and Scientific Advisory Committee to the All-Party Parliamentary Pro-Life Group, London (Price: £2.50).

Flanagan, Geraldine Lux, *The First Nine Months of Life*, Life Cycle Books, Toronto (1962).

Verny, Dr Thomas with Kelly, John, *The Secret Life of the Unborn Child*, Sphere Books, London (1982), ISBN 0-7221-8821-8.

- *How You Began* SPUC Educational Research Trust, London (1991) (Price: 50p).

POPULATION

- Kasun, Jacqueline, *The War Against Population*, Ignatius Press, San Francisco (1988), ISBN 0-89870-191-0 (Price: £12.50).

Simon, Julian L., *Population Matters*, Transaction Publishers, New Brunswick, USA (1990), ISBN 0-88738-300-9 (Price: £24.95). Available from Committee on Population & The Economy, 53 Cavendish Road, London SW12 0DQ.

- Available from SPUC Educational Research Trust, 7 Tufton Street, London SW1P 3QN. Tel: 071 222 5845. Please add donations for postage.

Notes

1   The Church and the unborn child

1   *Westminster Confession* (1648), I:vi.

2   Middle Assyrian law, Law 53.

3   M. J. Gorman *Abortion and the Early Church*, Downers Grove, USA (1982), pp.33–4.

4   *Against Apion*, ii, 25, cited in G. J. Wenham, 'A Biblical theologian looks at abortion' in *Abortion: The Biblical and Medical Challenges*, London (1983) p.3.

5   R. F. R. Gardner, *Abortion: The Personal Dilemma*, Paternoster Press (1972), p.118.

6   The Didache II:1–2, English text in F. X. Glimm, *The Apostolic Fathers (Fathers of the Church*, vol. 1), Washington (1969), p.172.

7   John Stott, *Abortion*, Marshalls Paperbacks (1984), p.14.

8   Ibid., p.15.

9   Ibid., p.16.

10   Nigel M. de S. Cameron and Pamela F. Simms, *Abortion: the crisis in morals and medicine*, Inter-Varsity Press (1986), p.22.

11   David Braine, *Medical Ethics and Human Life*, Palladio Press, (1982), p.11.

12   The Didache, op. cit., p.172.

13   A. C. Coxe, *The Ante-Nicene Fathers*, vol. II, Michigan (1976), p.147.

14   S. P. Wood, *Clement of Alexandria: The Educator (Fathers of the Church*, vol. 23), Washington (1984), p.169.

15   P. Schaff, *Nicene and Post-Nicene Fathers of the Christian Church*, First series, XI, Michigan (1975), p.520.

16   A. C. Coxe, op. cit., vol. III, Michigan (1977), p.25.

17   Quoted in David Braine, op. cit., p.35.

18   St Augustine, *De Civitate Dei*, xxii.13.

19   James B. Nelson, 'Protestant Perspectives' in Warren T. Reich (ed.), *Encyclopedia of Bioethics*, vol. 1, Free Press, Illinois (1978).

20   John Calvin, *Commentary on the last four books of Moses*, vol. 3, trans. C. W. Bingham, Michigan (1973), pp.41-2.

21   Bernard N. Nathanson, *Aborting America*, Doubleday (1979), p.172.

22   Dietrich Bonhoeffer, *Ethics*, SCM, London (1955, 2nd impression 1971), pp.149–50.

23   Karl Barth, *Church Dogmatics*, vol. 3, 'The Doctrine of Creation', part 4. T. & T. Clark, Edinburgh (1961), p. 416.

24   Nigel M. de S. Cameron, *Is Life Really Sacred?*, Christian Action Research and Education, London (1989), p.36.

2 You knit me together

1 Margaret White, *Two Million Silent Killings*, Marshall Pickering (1987), pp. 15–16.
2 Sir William Liley quoted in Professor Jerome Lejeune and Professor Sir Albert William Liley, *The Tiniest Humans*, Robert Sassone (ed.) (1977) Library of Congress No. 77-76811, p.69. *The Tiniest Humans* is composed from transcripts of testimonies given by Professors Lejeune and Liley to: Sub-Committee on Constitutional Amendments of the Committee on the Judiciary, U.S. Senate, 93rd Congress, 2nd Session, 7 May 1974: and the Royal Commission on Contraception, Sterilisation and Abortion, New Zealand, 1977.
3 'Earliest feelings help to develop the senses', *New Scientist*, 7 May 1987, reviewing the research of Maria Fitzgerald published in *Nature*, 9 April 1987, vol. 326, p.603.
4 H. B. Valman and J. F. Pearson, 'What the Fetus Feels', *British Medical Journal*, 26 January 1980.
5 Peter McCullach, *The Fetus as Transplant Donor: Scientific, Social and Ethical Perspectives*, John Wiley and Sons (1987), p.132.
6 H. B. Valman and J. F. Pearson, op. cit.
7 Thomas Verny with John Kelly, *The Secret Life of the Unborn Child*, Sphere Books (1987), pp.7–8.
8 P. G. Hepper, 'Fetal "Soap" Addiction', *The Lancet*, 11 June 1988, p.1347.
9 Sir William Liley, 'The fetus as a personality', *Australian and New Zealand Journal of Psychiatry*, (1972), 6, pp.99–105.

3 Arguments for abortion

1 Edward Lenoski, *Heartbeat* vol.3, no.4, December 1980.
2 Sources: *Trends in Child Abuse 1977–1982*, NSPCC, 1984; *Child Abuse Trends in England and Wales 1983–87*, NSPCC, 1989; *Child Abuse Trends in England and Wales 1988–90*, NSPCC, 1992.
3 'Legalized Abortion: Report by the Council of the Royal College of Obstetricians and Gynaecologists', *British Medical Journal*, 2 April 1966, 1, pp.850–4.
4 *World Health Statistics Report*, vol. 30, no. 4 (1977), World Health Organisation, Geneva and *World Health Statistics Annual*, WHO, Geneva, various editions.
5 *Report of the Committee on the Working of the Abortion Act (The Lane Report)* HMSO, London, April 1974, vol. II, p.4.
6 Department of Health, *Report on Confidential Enquiries into Maternal Deaths in England and Wales 1979–81* and *1982–4*.
7 House of Commons *Hansard*, col. 276, 17 January 1990.
8 *World Health Statistics Annual*, WHO, Geneva, various editions.
9 *The Times*, 9 November 1982.
10 World Health Organisation, *World Health Statistics Annual*, Geneva, 1985.
11 Henry Redhead, *A Letter to Bache Heathcote Esq on the fatal consequences of abolishing the slave trade both to England and her American colonies*, London (1792), p.55.
12 Bryan Edwards, speaking at a meeting of the Joint Committee of the Council and Assembly of Jamaica, 19 September 1789, quoted in Averil Mackenzie-Grieve, *The Last Years of the English Slave Trade; Liverpool 1750–1807*, Frank Cass & Co., London (1968), p. 239.
13 Captain Crow of the *Kitty's Amelia*, quoted in Christopher Lloyd, *The Navy and the Slave*

Trade: The Suppression of the African Slave Trade in the Nineteenth Century, Longmans Green and Co. (1949), p.8.

14 Wilberforce's speech is described in Robin Furneaux, *William Wilberforce*, Hamish Hamilton (1974), p.87.

15 *Hansard* 8, 975. Quoted in Robin Furneaux, op. cit., p.252.

16 Tertullian, *De Anima: A Tradition on the Soul*, cited in Jacob Viner, *Religious Thought and Economic Society*, Durham, Duke University Press, 1978, p.34.

17 Jerome, *The Principal Works*, cited in Viner, op. cit., pp.33–4.

18 Jacqueline Kasun, *The War Against Population: The Economics and Ideology of World Population Control*, Ignatius Press, San Francisco (1988), p.37; see also Jacqueline Kasun, *Population and the Environment; Debunking the Myths*, Population Research Institute, Baltimore, p.14.

19 P. R. Bibby and J. W. Shepherd, *Rates of Urbanization in England 1981–2001*, Department of the Environment Planning Research Programme, London, HMSO (1990), p.ix.

20 Speech by Barber Conable, President of the World Bank, to the Members' Assembly of the International Planned Parenthood Federation, reprinted in *People*, vol. 17, no. 2, IPPF, London (1990).

21 Ester Boserup, *The Conditions of Agricultural Growth: the economics of agrarian change under population pressure*, Earthscan Publications, 1993, pp.72,73.

22 Mary Tiffen and Michael Mortimore, 'Environment, Population Growth and Productivity in Kenya: A Case Study of Machakos District', *Development Policy Review*, vol. 10, No. 4, Overseas Development Institute, December 1992, p.382.

23 Donella Meadows, Dennis Meadows, Jorgen Randers, William Behrens III, *The Limits to Growth*, Potomac Association, New York (1972).

24 Working Group on Population Growth and Economic Development, U.S. National Academy of Sciences, *Population Growth and Economic Development: Policy Questions*, National Academy Press, Washington (1986), pp.15–16, 17.

25 *Population, Environment and Development; an issues paper for the third UNCED preparatory committee*, prepared by the Overseas Development Administration of the UK Government (1991).

26 Arthur Kay, 'When Green is Red', *Calvinism Today*, January 1991.

27 David Carter, 'Unnumbered blessings', *Third Way*, October 1991.

28 House of Lords *Hansard*, col. 1021, 7 December 1989.

29 Mandy Coates, *Christianity and Abortion: The Arguments of Pro-Choice Christians*, National Abortion Campaign, 1993, p.11.

30 R. F. R. Gardner, *Abortion: The Personal Dilemma*, Paternoster Press (1972), p.126.

31 See Winter's essay in *Abortion: the biblical and medical challenges*, Gordon Wenham and Richard Winter, CARE Trust (1983) p.13.

32 R. F. R. Gardner, op. cit., p.126.

33 Ibid., p.124.

34 D. Gareth Jones, *Brave New People: ethical issues at the commencement of life*, Inter-Varsity Press (1984).

35 D. Gareth Jones, *Manufacturing Humans: the challenge of the new reproductive technologies*, Inter-Varsity Press (1987).

36 Ibid., pp.151–2.

37 Ibid., p.154.
38 *Brave New People*, op. cit., p.163.
39 *Manufacturing Humans*, op. cit., p.152.
40 Ibid., p.153.
41 The confusion is similar to that in the argument that 'an embryo is only a potential human being' (see pp.102–3). In both cases the potential for something to develop while still remaining what it is already (as a small tree is potentially a large tree) is confused with the potential for something to become something else (as a tree is potentially paper).
42 *Manufacturing Humans*, op. cit., p.291.
43 Ibid., p.150.
44 Ibid., p.151, quoting E. A. Langerak.
45 Jones cites Peter Singer and Deane Wells as considering ovum, sperm and embryo to have the same status, and Michael Tooley as arguing that killing a neonate is no worse than killing a fetus, which is no worse than contraception. Ibid., pp.147–50.
46 *Prosōpon* and *panim* are not used in this way, nor is any other term. Indeed *prosōpon* and *panim* are sometimes used to refer to the face of non-persons (i.e. non-humans: animals and things). (See Gen. 1:2; Ezek. 41:19; Matt. 16:3.)
47 *Brave New People*, op. cit., p.169.
48 The development of Trinitarian doctrine, of course, made great use of the concept of 'person'. In this, the Latin word *persona* had as Greek equivalent both *hypostasis* (see Heb. 1:3) and *prosōpon*.
49 Oliver O'Donovan gives an excellent treatment of personhood using this approach in 'Again: Who Is a Person?' in J. H. Channer (ed.), *Abortion and the Sanctity of Human Life*, Paternoster Press (1985).

4 The hard cases

1 Robert Whelan (ed.), *Legal Abortion Examined*, SPUC Educational Research Trust, London (1992) pp.14–15.
2 Ibid. and *Abortion Statistics, England and Wales 1990* and *1991*, *Scottish Health Statistics 1991* and *1992*.
3 John F. Murphy and Kieran O'Driscoll, 'Therapeutic Abortion: The Medical Argument', *Irish Medical Journal*, 1982, vol. 75, no. 8, pp.304–6.
4 Professor James Fennelly, 'On the other hand: pregnancy and cancer', *Irish Times*, 29 June 1992.
5 M. P. Vessey and Sir Richard Doll FRS, 'Evaluation of existing methods: is the pill safe enough to continue using?' *Proceedings of the Royal Society*, series B, vol. 195 (1976) p. 73. Cf. S. D. Targum and N. H. Wright, 'Association of the intrauterine device and pelvic inflammatory disease: a retrospective pilot study', *American Journal of Epidemiology*, vol. 100 (1974) pp.262–71.
6 George Gordon, 'The lie that has stunned America', *The Daily Mail*, 10 September 1987.
7 The International Planned Parenthood Federation, which comprises member family planning/planned parenthood associations in 130 countries, gives detailed advice to its members on how to change laws which outlaw abortion. It advises associations operating in countries where abortion is restricted to give a 'broad' and 'positive' interpretation to any exclusion clauses in the law concerning risk to the mother's life or health, and to 'take up test

cases to pressurize for more liberal interpretation of some legislation'. ('Statement on unsafe abortion and reproductive health', *IPPF Medical Bulletin*, vol. 26, no. 1, February 1992).

8 Philip Ney and Adele Rose Wickett, 'Mental health and abortion: review and analysis', *Psychiatric Journal of the University of Ottawa*, vol. 14 (1989) pp.506–16; also H. N. Babikian, 'Abortion' in H. I. Kaplan and A. M. Freedman (eds.), *Comprehensive Handbook of Psychiatry*, 2nd ed. (1975), pp.1496–1500; M. Sim and R. Neisser, 'Post-Abortive Psychoses: A Report from Two Centers', in David Mall and Walter F. Watts (eds.), *The Psychological Aspects of Abortion*, Washington, University Publications of America (1979), pp.1–3; L. Appleby, 'Suicide during pregnancy and in the first post-natal year', *British Medical Journal*, 302: 137–140 (1991).

9 Sandra K. Mahkorn and William V. Dolan, 'Sexual Assault and Pregnancy', *New Perspectives on Human Abortion*, University Publications of America (1981), pp.182–99.

10 Dr and Mrs J. C. Willke, *Abortion: Questions and Answers*, Hayes Publishing Co, Ohio (1990) p. 155 citing Sandra K. Mahkorn, 'Pregnancy and Sexual Assault', *The Psychological Aspects of Abortion, op. cit.*, pp.53–72.

11 John Powell, *Abortion: The Silent Holocaust*, Argus Communications, Texas (1981), p.122.

12 Dr and Mrs J. C. Willke, *Abortion: Questions and Answers*, Hayes Publishing Co. Inc., Cincinatti (1990), p.157.

13 George E. Maloof, 'The Consequences of Incest', *The Psychological Aspects of Abortion*, op. cit., p.100.

14 F. LaGard Smith, *When Choice Becomes God*, Harvest House Publishers, Eugene, Oregon (1990), p.192.

5 Abortion and the law

1 Henry de Bracton, *De Legibus et Consuetudinibus Angliae*.

2 Aleck Bourne, letter to Colin Oliver, 15 February 1969.

3 See note 8 to chapter 4, above.

4 David Steel, House of Commons *Hansard*, vol. 732, col. 1075, 22 July 1966.

5 Cf. Dr David Owen MP: 'We should think of the doctor who is faced with the problem of a woman with seven children who tells him that she shares a bed with her husband and two children, with perhaps two other children living and sleeping in the same room', House of Commons *Hansard*, vol. 732, col.1114, 22 July 1966. Renee Short MP: 'The majority of women seeking termination of pregnancy are married women with too many children', ibid., col. 1163; Lord Silkin, sponsor of the Abortion Act (1967): 'It is probable that . . . four out of five are women who are in their late thirties or early forties, who already have an existing family of children, some of them grown up, and who, by reason of their domestic circumstances, just cannot face having another child', House of Lords, *Hansard*, col. 263, 19 July 1967.

6 Even the supporters of the 1967 Act no longer deny that it has given us abortion on demand. In proposing an amendment to the law to allow abortion on request up to 12 weeks, pro-abortion MP Emma Nicholson stated: 'The Committee should step away immediately from the fiction that the 1967 Act does not provide abortions on request – of course it does. The woman requests that abortion. Abortion on demand is just a more fearful way of describing abortion on request. General practitioners in my constituency and elsewhere tell

me that it is virtually impossible for a doctor to refuse an abortion under the workings of the 1967 Act', House of Commons *Hansard*, cols. 249/250, 24 April 1990.

7 Robert Whelan (ed.), *Legal Abortion Examined: 21 Years of Abortion Statistics*, SPUC Educational Research Trust, London (1992).

8 All members of the committee were initially favourably disposed towards embryo research, but a number became more and more perturbed during their researches and finally a group produced a minority report opposing the use of the human embryo for experiments.

9 Nicholas Timmins, 'Embryos: The Case for Research', *The Times*, 26 June 1984.

10 M. C. Macnaughton, *Embryo Research*, Royal College of Obstetricians and Gynaecologists, 15 January 1985.

11 *Freedom to Choose; Research into Infertility and Congenital Handicap*, PROGRESS pamphlet, London, 1989, p.9.

12 Professor Jerome Lejeune, Letters, *The Times*, 26 March 1985.

13 Professor R. B. Zachary, 'Life with spina bifida', *British Medical Journal*, 3 December 1977.

14 Judge's summing up in the trial of Dr Leonard Arthur, 5 November 1981.

15 'Consultants working in neo-natal intensive care units are faced with the decision at least a dozen times a year of whether to allow a severely handicapped baby to die. Dr Malcolm Chiswick of St Mary's Hospital, Manchester, said the decision was always made jointly between the parents and the consultants and happened in his unit at least once a month.' ('Doctors facing monthly life or death dilemma', *The Sunday Telegraph*, 21 October 1990); 'Professor Peter Dunn, head of the department of perinatal medicine at the University of Bristol . . . said he dealt with at least one baby a month who was so severely handicapped it was allowed to die.' ('Head of LIFE offers to look after Baby J', *The Sunday Correspondent*, 21 October 1990); 'The condition of Baby J, if he lived, would be similar to that of the severe spina bifida children whom doctors were able to save from the mid-1960s onwards, explained Dr Nicholson. Those babies were not now kept alive because doctors realised that their quality of life would be appalling'. ('Handicapped baby may be left to die say judges', *The Daily Telegraph*, 20 October 1990).

16 Quoted in Francis A. Schaeffer and C. Everett Koop, *Whatever Happened to the Human Race?* Marshall Morgan Scott (1980), p.53.

17 *BMA News Review*, January 1993.

18 *The Times*, 16 December 1992.

19 Karl Binding and Alfred Hoche, *Die Freigabe der Vernichtung lebensunwerten Leben: Ihr Mass und ihre Form (The permission to destroy life unworthy of life)*, F. Meiner, Leipzig (1920).

20 Ibid.

21 Gerhard Schmidt, *Selektion in der Heilanstalt 1939-1945, (Selection in the Health Institute)* Evangelisches Verlagsanstalt, Stuttgart (1965), pp.34–5.

6 Abortion and the doctors

1 *Le Quotidien de Medecine*, 30 April 1990.

2 P. Coles, quoting R. Henrion in *Nature*, vol. 335, 6 October 1988.

3 A. Templeton, quoted in *The Times*, 27 October 1989.

4 Germaine Greer, *Sex and Destiny*, Secker and Warburg, 1984, p.163.

5 Ibid., p.171.

6   Written answer, *Hansard*, cols 238–9, 10 May 1983.

7   John Finnis, 'The Meaning of Miscarriage' in the *Newsletter* of the Association of Lawyers for the Defence of the Unborn, no. 19, Autumn 1983.

8   P. I. Frank et al., 'Induced abortion operations and their early sequelae', *Journal of the Royal College of General Practitioners* (1985), 35:175-80.
    Major complications were defined as:
    a. Death (none occurred in the study)
    b. Haemorrhage of 500ml or more or requiring blood transfusion
    c. Uterine perforation
    d. Complications necessitating laparotomy
    e. Salpingitis
    f. Pulmonary embolism (i.e. blood clots breaking off and moving to the lungs)
    g. Cerebrovascular morbidity (i.e. strokes)
    h. Deep vein thrombosis of legs (patients are at risk of pulmonary embolism)
    i. Psychosis.

9   L. Heisterberg and M. Kringelbach, 'Early complications after induced first trimester abortion', *Acta Obstetrica et Gynaecologica Scandinavica* (1987), 66(3):201–4.

10 S. Linn et al., 'The relationship between induced abortion and outcome of subsequent pregnancies', *American Journal of Obstetrics and Gynaecology* (1983), 15 May, 146(2):136–40.

11 A. Peterlin and L. Andolsek, 'The effect of induced abortion in adolescence on the manifestations of spontaneous abortion, premature labor and birth weight', *Jugoslavenska Ginekologija i Perinatolgija* (1986) May–Aug; 26(3–4):49–52.

12 F. E. Skjeldestad, 'Induced abortion: chlamydia trachomatis and postabortal complications. A cost benefit analysis', *Acta Obstetrica et Gynaecologica Scandinavica* (1988); 67(6):525–9; and S. J. Duthie et al., 'Morbidity after termination of pregnancy in first trimester', *Genitourinary Medicine* (1987), 63:182–7.

13 J. Malcolm Pearce, 'Pelvic Inflammatory Disease', *British Medical Journal* (1990), vol. 300, pp.1090–1.

14 *Ciba Foundation Symposium* (1985), vol. 115, pp.150–61.

15 G. Zolese & C. V. R. Blacker, 'The Psychological Complications of Therapeutic Abortion', *British Journal of Psychiatry* (1992), vol. 160, pp.742–74.

7   Research on humans

1   Robert Edwards and Patrick Steptoe, *A Matter of Life*, Hutchinson (1980), p.39.

2   cited in ibid., p.85.

3   Dr Michael Hall of Roche Pharmaceutical Company, quoted in 'AIDS technique has potential of producing people to order', *The Guardian*, 26 August 1987.

4   K. L. Moore, *The Developing Human*, W. B. Saunders (1988), p.1.

5   Ibid., p.437.

6   Dr W. D. Richardson, 'Growth control in the developing central nervous system', *MRC News*, March 1990, p.6.

7   Dr R. J. Aitken, 'Development of contraceptive vaccine', Ibid., p.28.

8   The Warnock Committee, *Report of the Committee of Inquiry into Human Fertilisation and Embryology*, London (1984), HMSO, p.60.

9 Robert Edwards, *Life Before Birth*, Hutchinson (1981), p.53.

10 House of Lords *Hansard*, col. 1020, 7 December 1989.

11 Nigel Cameron, editorial, *Ethics and Medicine* (1990), 6.1.

12 *Warnock Report*, op. cit., p.65.

13 Ibid., p.66.

14 Patricia Spallone, *Beyond Conception: The New Politics of Reproduction*, Macmillan (1989), pp.53,207.

15 *Nature*, Correspondence, vol. 320, 20 March 1986, p.208.

16 *Nature*, Editorial, 14 May 1987.

17 Royal College of Obstetricians and Gynaecologists, *Statement on assisted reproduction (pre-implantation embryo) and embryo research*, December 1989; Medical Research Council *Legislation on human infertility services and embryo research – a consultation paper*, 1987, p.5.; House of Lords, *Hansard*, col. 1054, 7 December 1989.

18 Ibid., col. 1021.

19 John McLean, 'Early Human Embryo Loss' in *Upholding Human Dignity*, The Parliamentary Medical and Scientific Advisory Committee to the All-Party Parliamentary Pro-Life Group, London (1989), pp.23–7.

20 P. G. Whittaker, A. Taylor, T. Lind, 'Unsuspected pregnancy loss in healthy women', *The Lancet* (1983), 1, pp.1126–7.

21 House of Lords *Hansard*, col. 957, 8 February 1990.

22 *The Warnock Report*, op. cit., p.61.

23 E. O. Wilson, *On Human Nature*, Bantam Books (1978), p.54.

24 *Nature*, Correspondence, 2 July 1987, p.10.

25 House of Lords *Hansard*, col. 1026, 7 December 1989.

26 The father of adult twins, both suffering from cystic fibrosis, wrote to the *Independent* (letters page, 27 November 1989) claiming that their 'one hope is a cure which embryonic research has brought in reach'. MENCAP issued a statement from Lynne Dodd whose daughter Kerida was described as 'severely mentally handicapped' with 'no speech, a club foot, partial vision, epilepsy, and a tendency to contract alimentary and urinary infections'. Mrs Dodd said, 'I love her, but I would give anything for her to have enjoyed a full life rather than the very limited life that she must lead'. Mrs Dodd clearly failed to appreciate that the aim of the embryo research she was defending would not have been a 'full life' for Kerida, but no life at all, as a result of genetic screening followed by abortion.

27 Leo Alexander, 'Medical Science Under Dictatorship', *New England Journal of Medicine*, 14 July 1949.

28 *Warnock Report*, op. cit. Eight of the report's thirteen chapter titles include the term 'infertility'.

29 Human Fertilisation and Embryology Authority, Second Annual Report, 1993: 12550 embryos were transferred to the womb in the 5 month period covered by the data in the report (August to December 1991). 897 of these babies survived beyond the perinatal period. See tables 1b page 17, and 5 page 19.

30 Progress – Campaign for Research into Reproduction, November 1985 newsletter.

31 See, for example, Patricia Spallone, *Beyond Conception*, Macmillan Education (1989), and Renate Klein, *The Exploitation of a Desire* Deakin University Press (1989).

8   Handicapped children

1   House of Lords *Hansard*, col. 1049, 18 October 1990.

2   Ann Shearer, *Disability: Whose Handicap?* Blackwell (1981).

3   For example: S. Dorner, 'Adolescents with spina bifida – How they see their situation', *Archives of Disease in Childhood*, 51 (1976); Stephen Kew, *Handicap and Family Crisis*, Pitman (1975); Mark Philip and Derek Duckworth, *Children with Disabilities and their Families, A Review of Research*, NFER (1982); B. Tew and K. M. Laurence, 'The Effect of Admission to Hospital and Surgery on Children with spina bifida', *Development Medicine and Child Neurology*, Supp.37 (1976); B. Tew and K. M. Laurence, 'Mothers, brothers and sisters of patients with spina bifida', *Development Medicine and Child Neurology*, Supp. 29 (1973); see also Erving Goffman, *Stigma: Notes on the Management of Spoiled Identity*, Pelican (1936).

4   Oliver O'Donovan, *Begotten or Made?*, Clarendon (1984).

5   Bernard Palmer (ed.), *Medicine & The Bible*, Paternoster Press in association with the Christian Medical Fellowship (1992).

6   Peter Singer and Helga Kuhse, *Should the Baby Live?*, OUP (1985) p.124.

7   Department of Health, *Prevention and Health: Everybody's Business: a reassessment of public and personal health* (1976) p.87.

8   Jeremy Laurance, 'London doctors make Down's breakthrough', *The Times*, 14 August 1992.

9   Richard West, *Born Imperfect: the role of genetic disease*, Office of Health Economics (1993), p.3.

10   Ibid., p.30.

11   Ibid., p.28.

12   Adolf Hitler, *Mein Kampf*, translated by James Murphy, Hurst and Blackett (1939) pp.338–9.

9   Abortion's other victims

1   G. Zolese & C. V. R. Blacker, 'The Psychological Complications of Therapeutic Abortion', *British Journal of Psychiatry*, vol. 160 (1992), pp.742-9.

2   E.g. E. de Carvalho and A. Monteiro, 'Rematrixing an experience with abortion', *Journal of Group Psychotherapy, Psychodrama and Sociometry* (1990), 43, pp.19–26; L. DeVerber et al., 'Post-abortion grief; psychological sequelae of induced abortion', *Humane Medicine* (1991), 7, pp.203–9; T. Steinberg, 'Abortion Counselling To Benefit Maternal Health', *American Journal of Law and Medicine* (1987), 15, pp.483–517; C. Barnard, *The Long Term Psychological Effect of Abortion*, Portsmouth, New Hampshire, Institute for Abortion Recovery and Research (1990).

3   E.g. Terry Selby and Marc Bockmon, *The Mourning After; Help for Post-abortion Syndrome*, Baker Book House, Grand Rapids, Michigan (1990); David Reardon, *Aborted Women; Silent No More*, Loyola University Press, Chicago (1987); Anne Speckhard, *The Psycho-Social Aspects of Stress Following Abortion*, Sheed and Ward, Kansas City (1987).

4   Lodi, McGettigan and Bucy, 'Women's response to abortion: implications for post-abortion support groups', *Journal of Social Work and Human Sexuality* (1985), 3, pp.119–32.

5   Philip Ney, 'Relationship between abortion and child abuse', *Canadian Journal of Psychiatry*, vol. 24 (1979), pp.610–20.

10 Christian responsibility in public affairs

1 J. R. W. Stott, *Issues Facing Christians Today*, Marshall Pickering (1984), p.6. Stott quotes David O. Moberg in *The Great Reversal*, Scripture Union (1973). The term was first used by the American historian Timothy L. Smith.

2 Francis A. Schaeffer and C. Everett Koop, *Whatever Happened to the Human Race?*, Marshall, Morgan and Scott (1980), p.152.

11 Our guilty silence

1 In February 1993 the General Synod of the Church of England passed a resolution on the subject of abortion which was the first for ten years. This lengthy resolution could manage no stronger statement about abortion than that it was 'a procedure which should not be undertaken lightly but only after the most serious moral reflection', and referred to occasions 'when abortion has to be undertaken'. A number of major denominations (e.g. the United Reformed Church and the Baptist Union) have produced no resolution or agreed statement.

2 The Methodist Statement on Abortion (adopted by the Methodist Conference of 1976) concedes only that 'every fetus has significance' and allows abortion as 'morally justifiable' in cases of handicap, large families, poverty and bad housing.

3 For example, virtually no publicity was given to the change in British law in 1990 that allowed abortion up to birth (see Chapter 5).

4 The most extensive treatment of abortion in the broadcast media is probably in the many 'soap operas' that both reflect and shape popular culture. In one week in January 1993 three 'soaps' on network television had abortions in their storyline.

5 The situation is different in Northern Ireland.

6 Those belonging to Feminists Against Eugenics, for example, who can be contacted at 173 Minster Court, Liverpool L7 3QF.

7 More information about SPUC Evangelicals can be found in the Appendix. Other pro-life organisations also work from a specifically Christian basis – notably CARE (Christian Action Research and Education), 53 Romney Street, London SW1P 3RF and the Order of Christian Unity, 58 Hanover Gardens, London SE11 5TN.

8 SPUC can provide guidance for those needing help in this area.

9 It can be difficult for some, particularly in junior positions, to make such a refusal.

Index of Scriptural References

Index

refusal of ante-natal testing
109
and right to choose 28, 50
self-help networks 120–1

see also health effects; mother
World Bank 35
World Health Organisation
statistics 32

World Medical Association 89

zona pelucida 96
zygote 16, 91